DATE DUE			

3930013009

322
SHE

Sherrow, Victoria.

Separation of church
and state.

**PRAIRIE VIEW JUNIOR HIGH
TINLEY PARK IL 60477**

SEPARATION OF CHURCH AND STATE

VICTORIA SHERROW

IMPACT BOOK
FRANKLIN WATTS
NEW YORK   LONDON   TORONTO   SYDNEY

The summary of principles of the Williamsburg
Charter is reprinted courtesy of First Liberty
Institute at George Mason University.

Photographs copyright ©: Ed Burke/The Saratogian: p. 1; Picture
Group Inc.: pp. 2 top (John Nollendorf), 7 top (Bryce Flynn),
15 (Michael Patrick); North Wind Picture Archives: pp. 2 bottom,
3 top, 4 top; Historical Pictures Service, Chicago: pp. 3, 5; The Jewish
Publication Society (illustration by Richard Fish, reprinted from
Haym Salomon, Liberty's Son, by Shirley Milgrim): p. 4 bottom;
UPI/Bettmann Newsphotos: pp. 6 top, 13 bottom; Wide World Photos:
pp. 6 bottom, 7 bottom, 8 top, 9, 10, 11, 12; The Miami Herald
Publishing Company: p. 8 bottom; The Smithsonian Institution,
Washington, DC: p. 13 top; FYI Pictures: p. 14; Fellowship of
Christian Athletes: p. 16.

Library of Congress Cataloging-in-Publication Data

Sherrow, Victoria.
Separation of church and state / Victoria Sherrow.
p.   cm. — (An Impact book)
Includes bibliographical references and index.
Summary: Discusses the separation of church and state
throughout American history and various conflicts and
controversies the policy has caused.
ISBN 0-531-13000-2
1. Church and state—United States—History—Juvenile literature.
2. Religion and state—United States—History—Juvenile literature.
3. United States—Church history—Juvenile literature. 4. United
States—Religion—Juvenile literature.   [1. Church and state.
2. Freedom of religion.]   I. Title.
BR516.S48   1992
322'.1'0973—dc20   91-39770 CIP AC

CONTENTS

Congress shall make no law respecting an establishment of religion, or prohibiting the free exercise thereof; or abridging the freedom of speech, or of the press; or the right of the people peaceably to assemble, and to petition the Government for a redress of grievances.

—U.S. Constitution, Amendment I

No religious test shall ever be required as a qualification to any office or public trust under the United States.

—U.S. Constitution, Article VI

C H A P T E R 1

SEPARATION
OF CHURCH AND STATE:
AN AMERICAN LEGACY

A mural showing a Crucifixion scene had been in the auditorium of a public high school in Schuyler-ville, New York, since 1965, when in 1988 some parents asked the school to remove the 10- by 12-foot painting. They said it violated the First Amendment establishment clause, the principle of separation of church and state. The school board disagreed.

How did the parents and the school board reach their different viewpoints? The board said the mural, painted by a former student, did not promote religion, nor did its presence imply official support of a certain creed. The attorney for the school board said that the painting showed "man's inhumanity to man" and that other scenes in the painting—a man in chains and two others fighting with swords—were not inherently religious.[1]

The parents said the mural did imply a government endorsement of Christianity and of religion in general. They also said that students from non-Christian homes might feel confused and uncomfortable when they regularly saw this large mural hanging in a prominent place in their school.

In August 1990, a federal judge ruled in favor of the parents. He agreed that the mural sent "a message of government endorsement of Christianity" and violated the constitutional separation of church and state. The judge said the school should remove the mural.[2]

In 1985, Bridget Mergens, a senior at Westside High School in Omaha, Nebraska, asked her homeroom teacher, who was also the school principal, if her Bible discussion group could meet on school property after school hours. When he said no, she sued the school board.

Her lawyer argued that the school had violated the Equal Access Act of 1984, which forbids discrimination against student groups based upon their religious, political, or philosophical views. If chess and scuba clubs could meet after school, Bridget and her lawyer reasoned, Bible clubs should have the same right. Bridget lost her case in an Omaha federal court but won in the U.S. Court of Appeals. In 1990 the Supreme Court agreed with the Court of Appeals, saying that students' religious and political clubs can meet on the same basis as other extracurricular clubs.[3]

These cases reflect just two of the issues in the ongoing public debate about separation of church and state.

WHAT THE CONSTITUTION SAYS

At the founding of the United States, no country gave its people a written guarantee of freedom from government involvement in religion. The framers of the Constitution decided to do otherwise. They and the citizens who ratified it decided that religion was a personal rather than a political matter. Liberty of conscience—the right to follow the beliefs of one's choice—was regarded as a natural human right.

Article VI, Section 3, of the Constitution declares that "no religious test shall ever be required as a qualification to any office or public trust under the United States." In other words, a person may not be barred from holding political office on the basis of religion. Even more important, perhaps, are the first sixteen words of the First Amendment to the Constitution: "Congress shall make no law respecting an establishment of religion, or prohibiting the free exercise thereof."

THE IMPORTANCE OF SEPARATION OF CHURCH AND STATE

Many people call freedom of religion the most basic of all the liberties Americans enjoy. Constitutional scholar Leo Pfeffer calls it the forerunner of other liberties:

> *A government that will coerce its citizens in the domain of the spiritual will hardly hesitate to coerce them in the domain of the temporal. If it will direct how they shall worship, it will almost certainly direct how they shall vote.... Out of victory in the struggle for freedom to worship as one's conscience dictates came victory in the struggle for freedom to speak as one's reason dictates. Freedom of the press came from the struggle for freedom to print religious tracts, and freedom to assemble politically can be traced to the successful struggle for freedom to assemble religiously.*[4]

Besides being called a basis for other liberties, the separation of church and state has been cited as a reason for the strength of religious institutions in the United States. Americans are among the world's strongest supporters of houses of worship, with a high rate of membership, attendance, and financial support.

THE EFFECT OF THE COURTS

Many forces have shaped the American system of separation of church and state. In the two hundred years since the Bill of Rights was written, ideas about the relationship between government and religion have been reevaluated as the nation has grown, changed, and become more diverse. Often the opinions of groups and individuals have been in conflict. These conflicts are frequently resolved in the courts, as Americans seek redress for supposed wrongs—either too much separation or not enough.

The decisions that U.S. courts make about these differences of opinion affect our daily lives. They can determine what kinds of artwork may be placed in public schools as well as what kinds of clubs may meet in these buildings and at what time of day. They determine what textbooks are used in the schools and what subjects teachers may teach. They define what types of holiday displays will be placed in front of the town hall, how religious schools may use tax monies, and whether a state may force certain businesses to remain closed on Sunday.

As the final authority on constitutional issues, the Supreme Court must often resolve such disputes. In 1890, the Supreme Court gave a judicial definition of the word "religion" and set forth an early interpretation of the First Amendment religion clauses: "The First Amendment of the Constitution...was intended to allow everyone under the jurisdiction of the United States to entertain such notions respecting his relation to his Maker, and the duties they impose, as may be approved by his conscience, and to exhibit his sentiments in such form of worship as he may think proper, not injurious to the rights of others, and to prohibit legislation for the support of any religious tenets, or the modes of worship of any sect."[5]

In a famous 1947 case, the Court wrote an opinion regarded as the modern judicial interpretation of the First Amendment religion clauses:

> *Neither a state nor the Federal Government can set up a church. Neither can pass laws which aid one religion, aid all religions, or prefer one religion over another. Neither can force nor influence a person to go to or to remain away from church against his will or force him to profess a belief or disbelief in any religion. No person can be punished for entertaining or professing religious beliefs or disbeliefs, for church attendance or non-attendance. No tax in any amount, large or small, can be levied to support any religious activities or institutions, whatever they may be called, or whatever form they may adopt to teach or practice religion. Neither a state nor the Federal Government can, openly or secretly, participate in the affairs of any religious organizations or groups, and vice versa.[6]*

OPPOSING POINTS OF VIEW

People who want strict separation between religion and government have been called separationists; those who think that government and religious groups can work together are often called accommodationists. People also find that their opinions shift:

they may favor strict separation on one issue (e.g., prayer in schools) while favoring accommodation in another (e.g., tax exemptions for religious bodies.)

Some Americans believe the courts have gone too far in keeping government and religion separate. During his two terms in office (1980–1988), President Ronald Reagan was among those who supported a school prayer amendment to the Constitution. Many people who agree with this idea have denounced the 1962 and 1963 rulings that banned officials from composing or selecting prayers to be used in devotional exercises by children in public schools. Critics of this and other Supreme Court decisions say that the government has shown lack of interest in, even hostility toward, religion. Chief Justice William H. Rehnquist has said that the First Amendment does not forbid government from aiding religions as long as such aid is impartial.[7] Judge W. Brevard Hand, a federal district court judge in Alabama, believed in 1984 that his state could legally name an official religion.[8]

On the other side are those who think that government should be as neutral as possible regarding religion. They think that both religion and government function best when kept separate. The Reverend Dr. Robert L. Maddox, executive director of Americans United for Separation of Church and State, has said that separation of church and state is threatened when religious groups seek tax support for their schools and other activities. Separationists often claim that, throughout history, government involvement in religion has led to interference and persecution, especially of minorities. They point out that America is the most pluralistic country in the world, with a uniquely diverse population of different religious groups. Thus the government must be careful to be neutral in order not to offend the rights of the minority.

ISSUES IN SEARCH OF RESOLUTION

Conflicts regarding religion can be bitter and difficult to resolve. Should the Bible be read aloud in public schools? Should parochial schools receive public funding? Can an employee be fired for refusing to work on his or her Sabbath? The courts have wrestled with questions like these, striving to reconcile the rights of groups and individuals. Through the years, some citizens have endured criticism and long court battles as they challenged local, state, or federal practices that they thought were unconstitutional. These Americans have drawn public attention to religious discrimination and to government practices that promoted or hindered religions in questionable ways.

In this manner, "we the people" have given life to the words written in the Bill of Rights. As Justice Felix Frankfurter observed in 1948: "The Constitution is not something up there in the blue. It's down here, and we're living it and making it every day."[9]

CHAPTER 2

CHURCH AND STATE
IN
COLONIAL AMERICA

A visitor to the American colonies in the year 1770 would have found a number of different religious groups. Many early settlers, as well as many later immigrants, came to the land across the Atlantic for religious reasons. Some fled from religious discrimination or persecution in their homelands. Some disliked being forced to pay money to support government-sponsored or "established" religions. Others sought new territory where they could build a community for the members of their faith. These traits of the American settlers—dissent from established religions and political ideas, diverse religious beliefs, and strong interest in religion—helped to shape the nation's distinctive ideas about freedom and church-state relationships.

CHURCH-STATE RELATIONSHIPS IN THE OLD WORLD

Many early American colonists came from countries where church and government had been connected for centuries. What types of church-state relationships were part of this heritage?

Throughout history, religion and the state have often been intertwined. Ancient peoples living in Greece, Rome, and Israel were bound to support the religions of their rulers. Rulers of the Roman Empire persecuted Jews and early Christians when the latter refused to worship Roman gods and to provide money for Roman temples. Jews endured persecution and officially sanctioned discrimination in Europe and other places.

In the Middle Ages in Europe, the dominant Roman Catholic church sometimes was linked with government and sometimes was at odds with rulers. Church officials disagreed with civil rulers about who should make various laws. During a conflict with King Philip of France in 1302, Pope Boniface VIII issued the *Unam Sanctam*, which said that "for every creature it is altogether necessary for salvation to be subject to the Roman pontiff."[1] Later, King Philip imprisoned the pope. In other disputes, clergymen threatened to excommunicate, or exclude from church membership, rulers who did not follow their orders.[2]

From early times to the present, political power has enabled religious groups to punish people with whom they disagreed. Imprisonment, wars, inquisitions, the burning of heretics, and witch-hunts were some of the results. Looking back on the history of such events, Supreme Court Justice Hugo Black once said, "In efforts to force loyalty to whatever religious group happened to be on top and in league with the government of a particular time and place, men and women had been fined, cast in jail, cruelly tortured, and killed. Among the offenses for which these punishments had been inflicted were such things as speaking disrespectfully of the views of ministers of government-established churches, nonattendance at those churches, expressions of nonbelief in their doctrines, and failure to pay taxes and tithes to support them."[3]

During the Middle Ages, new religious groups formed in Europe. Growing nationalism in England, Germany, France, and other countries, along with disputes over certain teachings and practices of the Roman church, led to the Protestant Reformation of the 1500s. Some Protestant groups, such as German Lutherans, were approved of in their homelands. Other religious sects were barely tolerated or were openly disliked, persecuted, or exiled. In some countries each new ruler belonged to a different church and expected citizens to conform.

Between 1536 and 1540, the (Protestant) Church of England—the Anglican church—replaced Roman Catholicism as the official religion in Great Britain. By the early 1600s, every Christian country in Europe had an established church, either Protestant or Catholic. According to religious historian William Sweet, there was a widely held belief that "national safety and political unity depended upon religious uniformity."[4] In such an atmosphere, with a majority church in every area, the notion of separating church from state would have seemed strange indeed.

Meanwhile, new religious groups arose. In England, some people left the Anglican church to form Separatist and Puritan groups. Groups of these English Protestant dissenters were among the earliest and best known American colonists.

RELIGIOUS DIVERSITY IN COLONIAL AMERICA

Religious groups in the colonies were as varied as they were in Europe. In some places there was a multiplicity of groups and viewpoints. As the colonies grew, generally so did diversity—and the inevitable problems stemming from a mixture of people with different backgrounds and with different ideas about things.

In the Northeast, the Pilgrims, a small group of English dissenters from the Anglican church, settled in Plymouth, Massachusetts, in 1620. Their goal was to build a community where they could worship without interference. During the 1630s, another group of English dissenters, the Puritans, founded the Massachusetts Bay Colony near present-day Boston.

To the south, Dutch immigrants settled New Amsterdam (later renamed New York City) in the 1620s, where they started Dutch Reformed churches based on the Protestant teachings of John Calvin. The colony grew to become New Netherland (later New York State) and contained within it citizens from more than fourteen countries holding many beliefs. In addition to members of the Dutch Reformed, Anglican, and Catholic churches, there were Quakers, Lutherans, Presbyterians, Jews, and others.

In the southern colonies, immigrants loyal to the Anglican church settled in Jamestown, Virginia, chiefly for social and economic reasons. The southern colonists were a mixture of denominations. Anglicans and Huguenots (Protestant dissenters from the Catholic church in France) lived along the South Carolina coast. Scotch-Irish Presbyterians settled farther inland. In North Carolina, Anglicans lived along the coast, while Baptists, Presbyterians, Quakers, and others lived in the interior.

Georgia was the new home of various groups, including Austrian Salzburgers, a small group of Lutherans who had been ordered to leave their homes by a Catholic archbishop. Some Waldensians, members of Italy's oldest Protestant community, also founded a community in Georgia, as did Lutherans, Quakers, Catholics, Baptists, Anglicans, Moravians, Methodists, and Presbyterians.

RELIGIOUS INTOLERANCE IN THE COLONIES

Although many people settled in America to escape persecution in their homelands, quite a few of them brought with them prejudices similar to those that had driven them out of their homelands in the first place.

In the Massachusetts Bay Colony, citizens were legally bound to obey certain church rules. The Bay Colony did not tolerate people with other religious beliefs. Only church members could vote and have political privileges. Non-Puritans might be fined, imprisoned, beaten, or banished. Quakers were quite unwelcome: some were whipped or had their ears cut off. In 1659, two Quakers were hanged.

Puritans in Maryland passed laws in the 1650s denying freedom of worship and political rights to people associated with "popery or prelacy"— Catholics and Anglicans.[5]

Although Holland was known for religious tolerance, some early Dutch colonial leaders refused to let certain groups worship in public. When Peter Stuyvesant became director general of New Netherland in 1647, he decided to guide public morality by enforcing stricter religious rules. He also enforced discriminatory laws against Jews, Quakers, and Lutherans. However, his superiors in Holland, the directors of the Dutch West India Company, ordered him to follow more tolerant policies. They wrote, "The consciences of men ought to remain free and unshackled. Let every man remain free as long as he is modest, moderate, and his political conduct is irreproachable."[6]

RELIGIOUS ESTABLISHMENTS IN THE COLONIES

In Europe, established—government-sponsored—churches were the norm. They enjoyed formal recognition by law. One church was legally established in most countries. In America, by contrast, the different colonies developed a variety of relationships between religion and government.

Rhode Island separated these institutions from the outset. Pennsylvania, New Jersey, and Delaware either had no government-sponsored religions or disbanded them before 1776.

In contrast, the American colonies of Virginia, Maryland, North Carolina, South Carolina, and Georgia established the Anglican (later Episcopalian) church. The colonial governments gave the church special privileges, like financial support from taxes paid by all citizens.

Congregational (formerly Puritan) churches dominated in the New England states of Connecticut, Massachusetts, and New Hampshire. In Massachusetts in 1692, the government said that there was no official church, and yet each town was required to collect taxes from all residents to support a church chosen by popular vote. Boston was exempted from this law, because its Congregational church was already self-supporting. Those who attended other Boston churches could thus support their own church without paying taxes to another.

New York developed an unusual system, which has been called a multiple establishment of religion, or impartial support of Protestantism in general. After the English took over the colony of New Netherland from the Dutch, the Dutch Reformed church lost its guaranteed tax support. But all towns had to support a church and minister of a Protestant denomination of their choice.[7]

RELIGIOUS TOLERANCE IN THE OLD WORLD

The idea of separating church and state has been suggested throughout history. It perhaps originated with the New Testament words of Jesus Christ: "Render therefore unto Caesar the things which are Caesar's; and unto God the things that are God's" (Matthew 22:21). In the 1300s, Marsilius (Marsiglio), an Italian, proposed that the power of the Roman Catholic pope be limited to spiritual issues. Marsilius said that men are equal and that the state should get its power from those people whom it governs.[8] Nevertheless, religion and government remained intertwined.

In 1612, Thomas Helwys, regarded as the founder of the first Baptist church on English soil, declared that he had no intention of provoking evil against Roman Catholics, saying, "Wee do freely profess that our Lord the King hath no more power over their coonsciences [sic] than over ours, and that is none at all...let [people] be heretikes, Turks, Jews, or whatsoever, it apperteynes not to the earthly power to punish them in the least measure."[9] Other Baptists, living in exile in Holland during the early 1600s, agreed that no magistrate had the right "to meddle with religion or matters of conscience or compel men to this or that form of religion."[10]

RELIGIOUS TOLERANCE IN THE COLONIES: "DO UNTO OTHERS..."

In the colonies, with its great diversity, some people were bound to practice tolerance toward members of other sects. Sometimes, in fact, intolerance actually led to tolerance. Throughout the colonies, various official and unofficial acts paved the way for the development of a new attitude toward religion.

In Massachusetts an episode of religious intolerance sparked a unique colony, called by its founder a "livelie experiment." In midwinter 1635, Massachusetts Puritans exiled a dissenting preacher named Roger Williams. His wanderings led him to Rhode Island, where he formed the first community in modern times where church and state were officially separated, with freedom of conscience guaranteed. Clergyman Roger Williams considered religion a personal matter. While living in the Bay Colony, he had pressed for more democratic government, recommending that church and state function in separate spheres. Considered a heretic by some Puritans, Williams was exiled for his "new and dangerous opinions."[11]

Rhode Island offered religious and political liberty to all, including Native Americans. The charter said: "No person within the said Colony, at any time hereafter, shall be in any wise molested, punished, disquieted, or called in question for any differences in opinion in matters of religion."[12] Williams was also the first known person to describe a wall between church and state. He spoke of a "hedge or wall of separation between the garden of the church and the wilderness of the world."[13]

In 1657, Governor Stuyvesant of New Amsterdam received a letter from people who opposed his intolerant policies. "Any sons of Adam who come in love among us will be welcome," said a letter from the townspeople of Flushing, on Long Island. Their town charter contained a clause called "Freedom from Molestation," and the officials of Flushing vowed not to "condemn, punish, banish, prosecute, or lay violent hands upon anyone, in whatever name, form, or title he might appear."[14]

In Maryland, the first Lord Baltimore, George Calvert, offered English Catholics a refuge, along with immigrants of other faiths. Maryland's Act of Toleration (1649) forbade people to deride one another's beliefs or to use names such as "heretic," "papist," or "Puritan" to mock fellow colonists. The Act of Toleration further stated that civil authorities would be neutral toward Christian denominations. Raising the idea of "free exercise," the act said: "Nor [shall any be] compelled to the belief or exercise of any other religion against his or her consent."[15] This act protected many colonists but neglected non-Christians.

Not too many years later a man named William Penn told Native Americans living in the colony that became Pennsylvania: "The Great Spirit who made me and you knows that I and my friends have a hearty desire to live in peace and friendship with you…. It is not our custom to use hostile weapons against our fellow creatures, for which reason we have come unarmed."[16] Unlike some colonists, Penn regarded Native Americans as fellow human beings. His policies of fairness and nonviolence averted wars between settlers and Indians in Pennsylvania for seventy years.

An English aristocrat, Penn had received land in the New World from King Charles II in repayment of a debt and on it in 1682 had founded the colony of Pennsylvania. He called his plan of government a "holy experiment." The colony offered religious and political freedom and became the most religiously diverse of the thirteen colonies. Along with Quakers, Pennsylvania welcomed Puritans, Scotch-Irish Presbyterians, German Pietists and Anabaptists, Roman Catholics, Jews, Deists, Schwenckfelders, and people with no religious ties. Pacifist sects other than Quakers also settled there: Mennonites, Brethren (Dunkers), Amish, and Moravians. By 1776 there were about 403 different congregations in Pennsylvania.[17]

As the colonies grappled in their own ways with the problem of religion, changes also took place in England. English philosopher John Locke wrote his widely read *Letters on Toleration* in 1689, 1690, and 1692. Like many others, Locke said that true religious faith cannot be forced and that only a sincere voluntary belief has true religious meaning.[18] In 1689, Parliament passed the Act of Toleration, allowing Protestant dissenters to hold public services by registering their ministers and places of worship. But they could not hold public office, nor did the Act apply at all to Unitarians, Catholics, or Jews.

RELIGIOUS REVIVAL IN THE COLONIES

From the 1720s through the 1740s, America experienced a period of religious revival called the Great Awakening. Preachers visited different towns to preach lively sermons, often about the dangers of sin. There was more talk about religion, and some unaffiliated people joined churches.

The number of traveling ministers and revival meetings waned in the 1740s, but the Great Awakening had increased interest in Christianity. It also split several churches into new groups. The Presbyterian New School separated from the more conservative Old School. The Congregational church divided into evangelical and traditional groups. These events, along with increasing religious individualism, helped to further the idea of religious liberty for all.

COLONIAL LIFE-STYLES AND RELIGIOUS FREEDOM

Was uniformity of religion necessary to political and social unity? The early American settlers had a unique chance to put that question to the test.

Pennsylvania and Rhode Island had diverse populations, and yet they had avoided the religious persecutions common in Europe and were regarded as successful colonies. The lack of religious conformity did not shatter the social order.[19]

As a practical matter, it was important for colonists to get along. The settlers helped one another with many tasks, such as farming and defending themselves against Indians. Although some had come to America for religious reasons, others sought political freedom and economic opportunity. All tried to make their way in the colonies.

In America the need for labor outweighed the need for religious uniformity. People got to know members of religious groups that had been foreign to them. Sometimes a spirit of cooperation and fellowship resulted. During the late 1600s, Asser Levy, a Jew, helped some Lutherans build their first church in New York City.[20] During the Revolutionary War, several of Philadelphia's leading citizens helped to construct Mikveh Israel synagogue. Later the congregation of Mikveh Israel donated land for a Protestant church.[21]

The Revolutionary War brought diverse people together in support of common goals. Soldiers were of many different nationalities and religions. Many clergy, especially Presbyterians and Congregationalists, spoke out for independence. A number of minority faiths also opposed British rule. Independence carried with it chances for political, economic, and religious freedom.

Besides, the Revolution rested upon the idea that "all men are created equal." In early colonial days many members of minority groups who were used to harsh persecution may have been satisfied just to be allowed to build and attend their own churches. Later, Baptists, Catholics, Methodists, and others sought the same political rights the majority groups enjoyed. During the colonial period, every colony but Pennsylvania forbade the Catholic mass. Throughout the colonies, people had to pay taxes to support established churches. This made members of minority groups eager to fight for religious freedom.

However, the vast majority of colonists did not belong to any organized religion. Although there were many denominations, church and synagogue membership was small—estimated at between 4 and 8 percent of the population.[22] This is not to say that many colonists opposed religion. There were no organized churches or traveling ministers in many frontier areas, so people discontinued religious practices or carried on alone. Some settlers recalled unpleasant experiences with organized churches in their homelands and did not join a church in America. Others were preoccupied with day-to-day survival.

So a word that aptly describes American religious practices, even in colonial days, is *individualism*. People belonged to a variety of churches and synagogues, and many belonged to no religion at all. It is not surprising that under these conditions, the concept of religious liberty would grow. Some ideas that were gaining strength in Europe also helped strengthen the idea of freedom and diversity.

THE ENLIGHTENMENT

In Europe, the eighteenth century is often referred to as the Enlightenment, or the Age of Reason. During this period people began to examine human problems using scientific methods of thought developed during the seventeenth century. They questioned long-standing ideas about religion, politics, and economics and concluded that people could solve many problems by using their intellect and applying knowledge of natural science. Near the end of the colonial period, the ideas of European thinkers such as Voltaire, Diderot, and Descartes were widely discussed.

In America, Thomas Paine's 1776 pamphlet, *Common Sense*, sold hundreds of thousands of copies.[23] Paine discussed freedom from oppression in both politics and religion, saying, "As to religion, I hold it to be the indispensable duty of government to protect all conscientious professions thereof, and I know of no other business which government hath to do therewith."[24] Paine expressed ideas that would be echoed by some of the framers of the Bill of Rights. He suggested that a government should protect every citizen's right to believe as his or her conscience directs—but that is the government's only role with respect to religion.

The American nation developed its ideas about liberty in a unique setting during an era when the old ways were being reexamined. A growing population, diverse in religions and nationalities, and the practical needs of the colonies promoted the idea of religious tolerance—for how else could people from so many different groups live and work together in harmony? Growing individualism and new ideas about philosophy and politics expanded the idea of tolerance into what was at that time a radical idea: freedom of conscience for all.

After the Revolutionary War, a remarkable group of people assembled to shape these ideas into law. Under the Constitution and Bill of Rights, Americans would be promised religious liberty through a system that separated church and state.

C H A P T E R 3

CORNERSTONE OF RELIGIOUS LIBERTY: THE CONSTITUTION AND ITS AFTERMATH

Between 1776 and the Constitutional Convention of 1787, debates over separation of church and state took place in states that still had established churches. Virginia was the site of a fierce struggle between those who wanted to maintain the official Anglican church and those who wanted separation. Two political leaders of the group that urged separation were famous Virginians who would later strongly influence the U.S. Constitution: Thomas Jefferson and James Madison.

James Madison had played an important role in wording the Virginia State Bill of Rights in 1776. After George Mason drafted a clause that granted people "the fullest toleration in the free exercise of their religion," Madison asked him to change the words to say that all people were "equally entitled to the full and free exercise of their religion."[1] Madison found the word "toleration" condescending. He said, "The right of every man is liberty, not toleration."[2]

JEFFERSON'S BILL FOR RELIGIOUS FREEDOM

In 1782, Thomas Jefferson wrote that the govenment had no authority in the area of religion except to prevent "such acts only as are injurious to others."[3] He went on to say, "It is error alone that needs the support of government. Truth can stand on its own. Subject opinion to coercion: Who will you make your inquisitors? Fallible men; men governed by bad passions, by private as well as public reasons."[4]

Jefferson wrote his ideas about church-state separation in the Virginia Bill for Establishing Religious Freedom. The bill provided that nobody should be legally forced to attend or support a religious institution, nor should anyone suffer the loss of personal property or civil liberties because of religious beliefs and opinions. The bill was brought before the Virginia legislature but was not passed until several years later, when Jefferson's colleague, James Madison, led a successful struggle against an effort to give public taxes to religious institutions.

MADISON'S FIGHT AGAINST RELIGIOUS ASSESSMENTS

In 1785, James Madison urged his fellow Virginians "to take alarm at the first experiment on our liberties." He asked: "Who does not see that the same authority which can establish Christianity, in exclusion of all other Religions, may establish with the same ease any particular sect of Christians, in exclusion of all other sects? That the same authority which can force a citizen to contribute three pence only of his property for the support of any one establishment, may force him to conform to any other establishment in all cases whatsoever?"[5]

Madison, honored as the Father of the Constitution, wrote these words in his famous, often-quoted *Memorial and Remonstrance against Religious Assessments*. The *Remonstrance* sharply criticized Patrick Henry's proposal to use tax money to support teachers of the Christian religion in Virginia. In response to Henry's suggestion, Madison wrote, "Religion or the duty which we owe to our Creator, and the Manner of discharging it, can be directed only by reason and conviction, not by force or violence."[6] Madison warned that whatever religious group made up the majority might trespass on the freedom of religious minorities. The *Remonstrance* aroused public opinion against the assessment.

After considering the different viewpoints, the Virginia legislature passed Jefferson's Bill for Establishing Religious Freedom. By enacting the Statute for Religious Freedom in 1786, Virginia is thought to have become the first state in history to impose upon itself a law granting complete religious freedom and equality.[7] The statute also influenced the U.S. Constitution.

THE CONSTITUTIONAL CONVENTION

The fifty-five men who assembled in Philadelphia in 1787 to write the Constitution set out to shape a government unlike any that had previously existed. In search of "a more perfect union," they planned to limit the powers of the central government while still unifying the new nation. Unlike other governments at that time, the new United States government gave itself no control over religious matters.

Chief among the framers of the Constitution was James Madison, who believed that government interference with religion tended to harm both government and religion. He also believed that each religion should be supported by contributions made by members. Thomas Jefferson and other delegates to the Constitutional Convention shared Madison's views.

Records of discussions at the convention show that the delegates said little about religion. The Constitution itself contains no references to God or to a Supreme Being. The one reference to religious liberty appears in Article VI, which forbids religious tests as a qualification for public office. In other words, it says the government cannot require public servants to belong to a particular church or synagogue.

South Carolina delegate Charles Pinckney proposed a provision to forbid the use of religious tests in qualifying people for public office. His motion was passed, becoming Article VI, Clause 3, of the Constitution. Pinckney also supported an alternative to the oath that elected officials must take "to uphold the Constitution," specifying that Quakers and others who oppose oaths may substitute the word "affirm" for "swear." Article II, Section 1, Part 8, of the Constitution includes this provision. Pinckney further urged the adoption of an amendment saying that "the legislature of the United States shall pass no law on the subject of religion."[8] These were significant contributions to the American system of church-state separation.

THE BILL OF RIGHTS

During the Constitutional Convention, a number of delegates called for a Bill of Rights, a document that would state the basic rights belonging to the people. The motion was defeated. Some delegates thought a list of individual liberties was unnecessary because most states already had a bill of rights. Other people pointed out that the powers of government had been carefully limited by the Constitution. In regard to religious liberty, Madison said, "There is not a shadow of right in the general government to intermeddle with religion."[9] How could there be an abuse of power where none had been given?

But George Mason and other leaders and citizens urged that personal freedoms be listed and guaranteed. Shortly after George Washington's inauguration as president, James Madison announced that he would submit a Bill of Rights to Congress. Samuel Livermore of New Hampshire has been credited with suggesting the language that developed into the religion clauses of the First Amendment. He wrote: "Congress shall make no laws touching Religion, or infringing the rights of Conscience."[10] Various forms of the Amendment were suggested and discussed until the framers agreed upon the final wording: "Congress shall make no law respecting an establishment of religion or prohibiting the free exercise thereof; or abridging the freedom of speech, or of the press; or the right of the people peaceably to assemble, and to petition the Government for a redress of grievances." In December 1791 the state of Virginia ratified the Bill of Rights. The first ten amendments had gained the approval of eleven states and had become part of the U.S. Constitution.

EARLY INTERPRETATIONS OF THE RELIGION CLAUSES

How did the nation's first presidents interpret the religion clauses of the First Amendment? On the one hand, George Washington declared national days of prayer and approved the use of public funds to pay congressional chaplains. John Adams also declared national days of prayer and thanksgiving. On the other hand, James Madison and Thomas Jefferson said that the First Amendment prohibited them from proclaiming national days of thanksgiving, from exempting religious organizations from taxation, and from using government funds for any religious activities. Neither gave land grants to religious groups. Jefferson said that he would be violating the establishment clause of the First Amendment ("Congress shall make no law respecting an establishment of religion...") if he declared national days of prayer, even if they were nondenominational.[11]

While Jefferson was president, he used the oft-quoted phrase "wall of separation." In January 1802 the Connecticut Baptists Association of Danbury received a letter from President Jefferson. It said: "Believing with you that religion is a matter which lies solely between man and his God, that he owes account to none other for his faith or his worship, that the legislative powers of government reach actions only, and not opinions, I contemplate with sovereign reverence that act of the whole American people which declared that their legislature should 'make no law respecting an establishment of religion, or prohibiting the free exercise thereof,' thus building a wall of separation between Church and State."[12]

THE IMPACT OF THE FIRST AMENDMENT

When the Bill of Rights was drafted in 1789, there was much debate about the need for a strong central government versus the rights of individual states. James Madison and other early leaders had recommended that the federal Bill of Rights also be applied to the states, but that proposal was not adopted. Thus the adoption of the Bill of Rights did not automatically end all forms of religious discrimination and legal support of churches in every state. In fact, it applied only to actions of the federal government. The states could make different policies.

Some of these policies were liberal; others, restrictive. Some state constitutions granted personal freedoms similar to those in the federal Bill of Rights, most states exercised little control over individual faith and practice, and few states levied taxes to support religious activities. Yet religious restrictions remained in many state laws. Often these laws discriminated against Catholics, Jews, or other minorities and weren't changed until well into the nineteenth century—even into the twentieth century.

A Massachusetts law, repealed in 1833, for example, required each town to pay Protestant teachers to teach religion and morality. Only Protestants had full civil rights in New Jersey until 1844. Jews could not hold public office in North Carolina until 1868. Connecticut citizens' taxes helped to support the Congregational church until 1868. In New Hampshire, Jews and Catholics could not hold public office until 1876. Maryland did not grant full political rights to Jews and Unitarians until 1876.[13] Some such laws were not repealed until the 1900s. A long-standing law in Massachusetts imposed the death penalty for the crime of blasphemy—speaking disrespectfully about God or sacred things.[14]

Opposition to such laws came from both religious and political quarters. In Maryland, a Presbyterian named Thomas Kennedy urged the legislature to guarantee civil rights for Jewish citizens. Baptists and Quakers were among the other religious groups that worked to end discriminatory laws.

A FOREIGNER'S VIEW OF THE AMERICAN SYSTEM

In 1831 a Frenchman named Alexis de Tocqueville traveled throughout America. He wrote a famous book, *Democracy in America*, describing American life. At that time the American political system seemed strange and radical to many Europeans. De Tocqueville wrote that "the religious atmosphere of the country was the first thing that struck me on arrival in the United States." He found the situation unusual because, as he put it, "in France I had seen the spirits of religion and of freedom almost always marching in opposite directions. In America I found them intimately linked together in joint reign over the same land." After talking with a number of American clergymen and churchgoers, de Tocqueville concluded that the main reason for the high degree of religious participation in America was "the complete separation of church and state...throughout my stay in America I met nobody, lay or cleric, who did not agree about that."[15]

When de Tocqueville visited America, the majority of people still belonged to Christian religions, usually Protestant. In the decades that followed, millions of people of different faiths moved to America, seeking religious and political freedom. Yet many customs reflecting the Protestant beliefs held by most early colonists remained a part of American life and public institutions. As Americans became more diverse, conflicts over separation of church and state also increased.

CHAPTER 4

THE NINETEENTH CENTURY: CHURCH AND STATE IN CONFLICT

Between 1776 and 1820, about 250,000 people came to America. They included members of different Protestant religions, several thousand Roman Catholics, and a few hundred Jews, of whom about one hundred served in the Revolutionary War. During the rest of the 1800s, many additional groups settled in the United States, leading to a greater diversity than ever before. Many of these people came to the United States because of poor economic or repressive political conditions in their native lands. And mid-nineteenth-century America, in the midst of the Industrial Revolution, needed the additional labor and, despite some problems, benefited from the new blood.

Expanding borders offered fresh territory for settlement by groups and individuals. Among those who built new communities in the Midwest and West were different Protestant groups—Mennonites, Lutherans, Norwegian Quakers, Swedish Baptists— and non-Christians, including Jews from German-speaking countries. Mormons (members of the

Church of Jesus Christ of Latter-day Saints) and members of new sects that had begun in America, including the Holiness and Pentecostal groups, settled in western states.

During the late 1800s, more Catholics (from Ireland, Germany, and Eastern Europe) and members of the Eastern Orthodox church emigrated to America. Thousands of Jews from Eastern Europe and Russia arrived. Religious persecution in those countries eventually prompted one-third of the Jews to leave. About 70 percent of those who left Russia settled in the United States.[1] Also among the new immigrants from Europe were people with no religious affiliation.

THE CONCERNS OF MINORITY GROUPS

The arriving immigrants often had customs and beliefs that were different from those of people already living in America. Religious groups sometimes feared and mistrusted one another. Throughout the 1800s confrontations between religious groups were intense and, in some cases, violent.

The first major conflicts took place between Protestants and Catholics. As larger numbers of Catholic immigrants arrived in America during the 1800s, some Protestants feared that Catholics would gain too much control and influence, perhaps even involving the pope in American affairs. Unpleasant confrontations occurred in many cities, including, in 1834, Charleston, South Carolina, and Philadelphia.

The most heated conflicts involved public schools. In colonial days there had been few schools and no system of compulsory education. Many schools, especially those in New England, were church-affiliated and nearly always Protestant.

Some states required that teachers take oaths professing Protestant beliefs. As a school system strove to meet various new needs, including those of recent immigrants—like teaching them English and transmitting to them American cultural values—the original Protestant influence often remained. Since children spent a lot of time in school, many immigrants who did not share the beliefs of the mainstream Protestant majority began to object to the influence in the schools of that very same Protestant majority.

Catholic citizens were among those who opposed certain school religious practices such as Protestant-inspired Bible readings and prayers. In the 1850s, Bishop John Joseph Hughes of New York City complained that the Public School Society was "a completely Protestant organization that taught Protestant Christianity."[2] In order to avoid the Protestant customs that prevailed in many public schools, some Catholics started their own schools. They did not receive tax support, as did public schools, but in some places, Catholic schools asked legislatures for financial aid to buy their own textbooks and supplies. They did not want to use the Protestant-inspired textbooks.

Relationships between Protestants and Catholics were often tense. Some anti-Catholics formed secret societies like the Nativists and Know-Nothings, whose goals included keeping Catholics from being elected to public office. Catholics whose children remained in public schools protested when students had to participate in devotional exercises that included Protestant prayers and readings from the King James (Protestant) Bible.

Because they were a voting minority, Catholic citizens could not easily change the laws or strongly influence lawmakers, so they asked the courts for help. During one dispute, one hundred Catholic children were expelled from Boston schools for refusing to take part in religious exercises. Riots in Philadelphia led to injuries and deaths. In various cities, homes and church schools were burned. Mobs ordered Catholic priests to leave town.

Other groups also found that religious teachings in the schools conflicted with their beliefs. In 1843 some Jewish parents living in New York City complained that a textbook contained lessons based on the New Testament, which is not a part of the Jewish religion. The board of education refused to stop using the book. Showing a lack of understanding not unusual at that time, the board advised the Jewish parents not to be upset, because the lessons just "inculcate general principles of Christianity."[3]

Concerns of some minority groups rose in 1863 when a group of Protestant leaders founded the National Reform Association. One major aim of the organization was to add a "Christian amendment" to the U.S. Constitution. They also wanted the Preamble to the Constitution to be reworded so that it would begin with these words: "Recognizing Almighty God as the source of all authority and power in civil government, and acknowledging the Lord Jesus Christ as the governor among the nations, His revealed will as the supreme law of our land, in order to Constitute a Christian government."[4] Along with its supporters, the association worked for years to persuade Congress to adopt this proposal, but they did not succeed.

In the meantime, opponents of commonly accepted practices had few options. By protesting, members of minority groups might face ostracism by other community members. They also worried about whether their motives would be understood. Rabbi Arthur Gilbert writes about this issue from a Jewish perspective:

*There was a time...when Jews were too
frightened to litigate.... In former decisions,
the Supreme Court, and to an even greater
degree State Courts, had included assertions
that this was "a Christian nation" or "a religious country." Jewish opposition to religious
exercises in public schools and Christian
symbols on public property could easily be
misrepresented as an attack on religion and
Christianity. Reform Jews, particularly,
engaged in a major effort, utilizing the methods of education and persuasion, to sensitize
the conscience of Christian Americans, but
without significant results.* [5]

By the end of the nineteenth century, America had
larger numbers of people who did not share the
beliefs of the mainstream Protestant majority.
These people objected to the use of Protestant-based
prayers and oaths for public office. They especially
opposed the use of Protestant-inspired textbooks,
Bible readings, and prayers in public schools, where
their children spent a great deal of time.

THE FOURTEENTH AMENDMENT

Although groups and individuals wanted changes
in the way that government institutions promoted
or used religion, few people took their cases to court
during the nineteenth century. Often minority
groups were afraid of antagonizing the majority
groups in their communities. However, the main
obstacle was that before 1868, the Supreme Court
did not have the power to rule on many matters
that involved the separation of church and state.
The Bill of Rights, including the First Amendment
religion clauses, applied only to the national government, not to state and local practices.

In 1845, the U.S. Supreme Court made this point while issuing its first ruling in a fundamentally religious case. In *Permoli v. First Municipality No. 1 of New Orleans*, the Court was asked to decide whether the city of New Orleans could sustain a law making it illegal to expose a dead body, a law that city officials claimed was a public health measure. Opponents of the law said that not being able to expose a dead body in church for a funeral service violated their free exercise of religion. In the Court opinion, Justice John Catron wrote, "The Constitution of 1789 makes no provision for protecting the citizens of the respective states in their religious liberties; this is left to the state constitutions and laws."[6] Thus the Court did not rule for or against the New Orleans law, letting it stand.

All of that changed after Congress proposed the Fourteenth Amendment to the Constitution and the states ratified it in 1868. The relevant portion, contained in Section 1, states: "All persons born or naturalized in the United States, and subject to the jurisdiction thereof, are citizens of the United States and of the State wherein they reside. No state shall make or enforce any law which shall abridge the privileges or immunities of citizens of the United States; nor shall any state deprive any person of life, liberty, or property, without due process of law; nor deny to any person within its jurisdiction the equal protection of the laws."

The Fourteenth Amendment was drafted to protect the rights of black Americans after the Civil War, but it also enabled the Supreme Court to rule on state and local laws that people found to be in conflict with the Bill of Rights. The two clauses respecting "due process of law" and "equal protection of the laws" are often cited in cases concerning the Bill of Rights. By using the Fourteenth Amendment to apply the First Amendment to actions by states and communities, the Supreme Court could make decisions about state laws (for example, a law that forces businesses to close every Sunday) and on local practices (for example, the recitation of certain prayers in schools). Thus, along with actions of the federal government, after 1868, the actions of state governments, school boards, city councils, and other such agencies began to come under the scrutiny of the Supreme Court.

Many years would pass, however, before the Supreme Court considered its first case dealing squarely with separation of church and state. In the meantime certain issues began to emerge from the complex religious texture of the nation. These issues, tied to the various conflicts between religious groups, would take hold in the public consciousness and establish a legacy that would become ingrained in the American identity. Bible reading, school prayer, public displays of religious material, public aid for religious institutions—these were things that people were grappling with and that soon would become part of the domain of the various courts. Americans—new ones and old ones—were beginning to use some muscle in their attempts to enforce what they thought was not only right and just and fair but legal and constitutional as well.

RELIGIOUS OBSERVANCES IN PUBLIC SCHOOLS

In 1872, the Ohio State Supreme Court was asked to decide whether the Cincinnati Board of Education had the right to forbid the reading of the Bible in the city's public schools. The Cincinnati case arose after parents from different faiths protested religious readings in the schools. While the case was being decided, public opinion was sharply divided, and the vocal quarrels that ensued became known as the "Bible wars."

The court ruled that the board of education had the right to forbid Bible reading in Cincinnati schools. In rendering its opinion, the court made several comments strongly supporting separation between church and state:

Legal Christianity is a solecism, a contradiction in terms. When Christianity asks the aid of government beyond mere impartial protection, it denies itself. Its laws are divine, and not human. Its essential interests lie beyond the reach and range of human governments. United with government, religion never rises

*above the merest superstition; united with
religion, government never rises above the
merest despotism; and all history shows us
that the more widely and completely they are
separated, the better it is for both.*[1]

In 1910, the Illinois Supreme Court considered
another Bible reading case. In that case, some
Catholic parents asked that the schools be prohibited from having the Protestant Bible read during
the school day. The parents complained that
because school attendance was compulsory and no
other school was available, their children had to
attend a school where Protestant devotions were
held daily. In deciding to ban the readings, the
court said that "the exclusion of a pupil from this
part of the school exercise in which the rest of the
school joins, separates him from his fellows, puts
him in a class by himself, deprives him of his equality with the other pupils, subjects him to a religious
stigma, and places him at a disadvantage in the
school, which was never contemplated."[2]

THE U.S. SUPREME COURT JOINS THE FRAY

Around the nation, state courts reached various
conclusions about Bible reading during the early
1900s as citizens began increasingly to challenge
existing laws and practices. Other kinds of religious
issues reached the courts as well, but cases involving Bible reading were among the first to be litigated, and they continue to be litigated to this day.
Each state seemed to have something different to
say on the matter, and the U.S. Supreme Court had
yet to hear any cases.

In 1960, a survey showed that eleven states had
decided Bible reading was unconstitutional. Five

states had laws ordering that the Bible be read to all pupils. Seven states required that it be read, but let students be excused. Other states either let school districts make the decision or did not include any reference to school Bible reading in their laws.[3]

Finally, in 1963, a case involving Bible reading reached the U.S. Supreme Court. The case, *Abington School District v. Schempp*, had arisen in Pennsylvania. Unitarian parents Edward and Sydney Schempp had protested a state law requiring daily Bible reading in public schools. They argued that the material sometimes conflicted with their specific beliefs and that it was religious in nature, thus violating the separation of church and state. The school board argued that the Bible contained important moral lessons for students and that students could be excused from the exercise, which included recital of the Lord's Prayer, if they brought a written excuse from a parent or guardian.

The Supreme Court struck down the Pennsylvania law, ruling 8 to 1 that the Bible is indeed a religious book with a devotional character, so that reading it during formal periods in the school day is a religious exercise. The Court said that such devotional readings are an "establishment of religion" and thus unconstitutional in public schools.[4]

BIBLE READING: PRO AND CON

In spite of the Supreme Court ruling, the debate over Bible reading has never gone away. Supporters of Bible reading in public schools say that there are moral lessons in the Bible that teach values and build character and discipline. They say that schools should teach such lessons because some children do not get religious training at home. They contend that avoiding the use of the Bible in schools conveys a lack of interest in religion. In addition, supporters of this practice claim that beginning the school day with a recognition of God improves behavior. Finally, those who want Bible reading and devotional exercises in public schools claim that if most community members endorse these exercises, it is not fair for any minority to stop them. They claim that the Court has gone overboard in trying to prevent an "establishment of religion" and has, as a result, limited their "free exercise of religion."

Opponents of school Bible reading, including the American Civil Liberties Union and Americans United for the Separation of Church and State, point out that public schools are government institutions, supported by taxpayers of different beliefs. The schools serve a diverse group of children. Taxpayers and students should not have to support the religious beliefs of the officials who plan the exercises. Opponents also argue that different denominations use different versions and sections of the Bible or have their own sacred books, such as the Koran. By avoiding Bible reading and leaving worship services for the home and religious settings, public schools do not violate anyone's rights. Even if most community members want such exercises, say opponents, majority rule does not apply to religious issues, as it does in a political context.

Some religious leaders oppose devotional exercises in public schools, claiming that religion is degraded when it is used as a "tranquilizer" or a disciplinary technique. In *Abington v. Schempp*, Supreme Court Justice William Brennan quoted from *Christian Century* magazine: "An observance of this sort is likely to deteriorate quickly into an empty formality with little, if any, spiritual significance."[5]

Despite the decision in *Schempp,* Bible reading

didn't go away. In fact, as the years following this decision came to show, the idea of keeping Bible reading in the schools would prove so persistent that teachers, parents, administrators, school boards, state legislatures, governors, and others tried their best to look for ways around the law. And just as often, opponents of Bible reading would take them to court to demonstrate that "if it looks like a duck, walks like a duck, and quacks like a duck, it probably is a duck." Today Bible reading still takes place in some schools, primarily in southern states. For many, then, the issue is far from settled.

DISMISSED TIME FOR RELIGIOUS INSTRUCTION

When James Terry McCollum entered the fourth grade in 1945, he and his classmates were invited to enroll in the Champaign, Illinois, school system's released-time religious classes. His mother signed a permission card, designating Protestant classes, but after James attended the classes, his parents decided the teachings conflicted with the family's beliefs. The next year he did not enroll. As a result, James McCollum sat in the hall during religion classes or in a room near the teacher's bathroom and was told to read or keep busy until religion classes ended. Other students teased him.

In 1948, in *Illinois ex. rel. McCollum v. Board of Education*, the Supreme Court considered the constitutionality of the program. It noted that a private group hired and paid the religion teachers, who belonged to three different sects. School officials had final approval of the teachers. Roll was called, so the teachers knew who had attended the religion classes. The school provided space and worked closely with the religious bodies. It promoted the program, using class time to discuss it, pass out permission cards, and then collect them.

The Court decided 8 to 1 that this kind of activity by government (in the form of the school board) was an unconstitutional establishment of religion in the schools. Justice Hugo Black wrote, "Not only are the State's tax supported public school buildings used for the dissemination of religious doctrines. The State also affords sectarian groups an invaluable aid in that it helps to provide pupils for their religious classes through use of the state's compulsory public school machinery. This is not separation of Church and State."[6]

Justice Felix Frankfurter agreed, saying that young people feel a pressure to conform. Children who must declare their private, different religious beliefs in school may feel alienated. Frankfurter pointed out that religious disagreements can be bitter and divisive; thus, schools must stay nonsectarian in order to promote "cohesion among a heterogeneous, democratic people."[7]

The decision in *McCollum v. Board of Education* was scorned by some Americans and praised by others. During their years in court, the McCollum family endured harassing phone calls, malicious letters, physical attacks upon their home, and even death threats.[8] James's mother, Vashti, later wrote that she had been called "a wicked, godless woman, an emissary of Satan, a Communist, and a fiend in human form."[9] She explained that her goal was not to fight against all religion: "There is such a thing as indoctrination against religion as well as indoctrination for it, and I don't believe in either."[10]

An editorial in the *Chicago Sun-Times* had tried to calm some of the heated emotions by focusing on the issues involved: "The question to be decided is not atheism versus religious belief nor the value of religious education. The question is whether religious instruction shall be carried on in tax-supported public schools at which attendance is compulsory; and whether the type of instruction given semi-officially takes on, in practice, the form and substance of a compulsory curriculum."[11]

After the *McCollum* decision, school boards in other cities devised released-time plans that they hoped would be permissible. Four years later, in 1952, in *Zorach v. Clauson*, the U.S. Supreme Court had to decide if students could be dismissed early from school in order to attend religion classes *away from* school premises. In the majority opinion, Justice William O. Douglas wrote that this kind of program was an acceptable form of cooperation between schools and religious groups.

Not everyone agreed. Other justices noted that the schools remained open, and those students who did not attend religion classes were required to stay there. Justice Robert Jackson expressed concern that, in this type of dismissed-time program, the school "serves as a temporary jail for a student who will not go to church."[12]

Through the years, debates over Bible reading and released time and dismissed time for religious instruction have been intense. Yet these cases have caused less furor than the school prayer cases decided in the early 1960s.

PRAYER IN PUBLIC SCHOOLS: *ENGEL V. VITALE*

Can children legally pray in public schools? Yes, if they pray silently or in ways that do not disrupt school activities. But public school officials may no longer sponsor and lead group prayers, as they once did. Such religious exercises have been judged to violate First Amendment separation of church and state.

A major school prayer case, *Engel v. Vitale*, reached the Supreme Court in 1962. The New York State Board of Regents had written a brief prayer, which it regarded as nondenominational, and suggested that it be used in schools: "Almighty God, we acknowledge our dependence upon Thee, and we beg Thy blessings upon us, our parents, our teachers, and our country."

A Long Island school was among those that decided to have students recite this prayer daily. Several parents argued that the school board should not tell their children how and when to pray. The school board asserted that the prayer honored America's religious traditions and was not "compulsory"—a child could ask to be excused, then stand out in the hall during the exercise. William Butler, the attorney for the parent group, later said, "My argument with the state was that it was composing its own prayer and inserting it in compulsory institutions which will act as its churches and led by teachers who act as priests. So you have all the components of the establishment of religion."[13]

In response to the argument that students could be excused, the plaintiffs said that children fear being set apart from the group and would rather imitate others than risk embarrassment. The Supreme Court sided with the parents. Aware that some Americans might interpret its decision as being antireligious, Justice Hugo Black carefully explained the Court's position: "It is neither sacrilegious nor antireligious to say that each separate government in this country should stay out of the business of writing or sanctioning official prayers and leave that purely religious function to the people themselves and to those the people choose to look to for religious guidance."[14] The Court also emphasized that students can recite historical documents containing religious references and sing patriotic songs in which the composers profess religious beliefs.[15]

Still, public reactions were intense. Newspaper headlines said: "School Prayer Unconstitutional,"

"Ban Prayer in Public Schools," "School Prayer Held Illegal." Clergy members claimed to be shocked and frightened. One church posted a sign saying: CONGRATULATIONS, KHRUSHCHEV.[16] Many people misunderstood the decision, not realizing that silent, voluntary prayer by any American was not at stake. President John F. Kennedy made a statement acknowledging the different viewpoints but supporting the Court decision: "We have in this case a very easy remedy and that is to pray ourselves. And I would think that it would be a welcome reminder to every American family that we can pray a good deal more at home, and we can attend our churches with a good deal more fidelity, and we can make the true meaning of prayer much more important in the lives of all our children."[17]

After the case, the Supreme Court received hundreds of letters, mostly negative. In the two houses of Congress, 177 bills designed to cancel the Court's ruling were introduced. A school prayer amendment to the Constitution was proposed but never received enough votes to become law. In congressional hearings, prominent members of the clergy spoke against the amendment. The National Council of Churches, the largest Protestant group in the United States, also opposed it. Opponents said that good education did not require devotional exercises in public schools and that religion can be promoted at home and in houses of worship.

Still the arguments went on, and the issue became more politicized. The Republican party platform of 1980 voiced support for a school prayer amendment, and many schools defied the Court decision.

SCHOOL PRAYER: *WALLACE V. JAFFREE*

In 1985, another school prayer case, *Wallace v. Jaffree*, came before the Supreme Court. Alabama resident Ishmael Jaffree had complained that teachers in his children's elementary school classrooms led daily prayers. Letters and phone calls to school officials failed to end the religious exercises, so Mr. Jaffree filed a lawsuit.

At the trial, Mr. Jaffree said that his children were learning one thing at home and another at school. He said he thought children "on their own should be free to pray before meals, any time they want to" but that teachers should not tell them what to believe about religion or lead them in public prayers.[18] After Mr. Jaffree won his case in federal court, Alabama appealed to the Supreme Court, defending a more narrow law that allowed *silent* prayer. During the hearing, Justice Thurgood Marshall pointed out that students do not need legal permission to pray silently.[19]

The Supreme Court ruled in Jaffree's favor, saying that the state law permitting silent prayer was not constitutional. In the opinion, Justice Sandra Day O'Connor said that "excusing" students is not an adequate solution and that it sends the wrong message—"they are outsiders, not full members of the political community."[20] Ishmael Jaffree, who was born in Cleveland, Ohio, later wrote: "I got portrayed as a person who was trying to take God out of the public schools. The talk show in Mobile was filled with people who said, 'Why doesn't he go back to Africa where he came from?' I got all kinds of nasty letters, and I got nasty phone calls at all times of night. I used to talk with people and try to let them understand why I did this—that it was a matter of principle and the schools shouldn't be promoting anybody's religion."[21]

Opponents of the *Jaffree* decision complained that a minority of citizens was keeping the majority from praying aloud. They said that by removing school-sponsored prayers, schools promote "secular humanism"—a term that has come to mean a belief system that does not include worship of a Supreme Being or traditional religious ideas about supernatural powers.

Supporting the decision, a *Washington Post* editorial said, "Prayer is personal, private, and protected. Nothing prevents an individual child from praying silently in any place at any time."[22] The *Kansas City Times* said, "Well-meaning people who propose school prayer are fervent disciples of various sects and orders. So strong is their faith that they cannot understand why all do not wish to share in their vision. But there are many visions, and while the Constitution guarantees the right to pursue any or all, it does not permit the state to compel the pursuit of any or all.... In other times and even now in other lands, refusal to conform with religious law is dealt with severely. The U.S. wants none of it."[23]

However, other people sided with the three Supreme Court Justices who dissented in the *Jaffree* case. Chief Justice Warren Burger said that silent, voluntary prayer in schools was no threat to religious liberty.[24] And Justice William Rehnquist, who wrote a twenty-four-page opinion, said that the purpose of the First Amendment religion clauses had been merely "to prevent the establishment of a national religion or the governmental preference of one religion over another."[25] Criticizing the decision, *Washington Post* columnist John Lofton said that the Court had "sided with the village atheist in the name of neutrality."[26]

THE CONTINUING DEBATE ABOUT SCHOOL PRAYER

For some people, religious freedom means being able to have definite time set aside to pray in school. Justice Potter Stewart, the one dissenter in the 1962 *Engel* school prayer case, spoke for many others when he favored the idea of "letting those who want to say a prayer say it." He further said that not letting children recite a prayer in school "is to deny them the opportunity of sharing in the spiritual heritage of our Nation."[27]

For other people, the opinion of historian Samuel Rabinove reflects their views:

> *There is nothing in any U.S. Supreme Court ruling to stop a pupil from saying a prayer, either spoken or silent, any time the spirit moves him or her to do so, provided only that normal school activity is not disrupted thereby. Why, then, this virtual obsession with organized prayer during the school day? Few adults, after all, expect to be able to engage in organized prayer at their places of work during the work day. Parents for whom it is important that their children pray while in school are free to instruct them accordingly. What is really sought here...is induced prayer by* other *people's children, whether or not this is desired by* other *parents.*[28]

People are still debating school prayer issues. Despite clear support from President Ronald Reagan during his term (1980–1988), no school prayer amendment has been passed by Congress. Yet some teachers still lead prayers in classrooms, and officials say prayers at school-sponsored events such as football games.

In 1988, a Georgia court ruled that prayers before public school football games violate separation of church and state. Yet towns in Georgia, Florida, and Alabama continue to sponsor pregame prayers. A Georgia radio-station official described the strong feelings that some citizens have about this tradition: "The issue of prayer has nothing to do with football; football's caught in the middle. The issue is being able to pray at public events. It was something that struck very deep."[29]

HOLIDAY OBSERVANCES IN SCHOOLS

As public school officials have struggled with the issues of prayers and Bible reading, they also have debated how to observe holidays, especially Christmas. Some U.S. schools have traditional religious pageants, songs, and decorations. Should such religious themes be part of holiday celebrations in public schools?

In 1963, the United Presbyterian church addressed the subject, saying, "United Presbyterians actively strive to recapture from popular custom the observance of religious holidays in order to restore their deepest religious meaning." The organization said that mixing seasonal symbols such as Frosty the Snowman with religious ones in public schools reduces the sacred meaning of religious symbols. The church suggested that religious holidays be explained but not celebrated religiously and that students of various religious faiths should be given time off from school to celebrate important religious holidays with their families.[30]

Schools have worked out a variety of approaches. Some do not sing religious songs or hold religious functions at Christmas. Vacations scheduled at this time are now often called "winter vacations." Other schools sing songs from different religious traditions. In still other schools—usually in towns where religious beliefs are more uniform—carols, pageants, and other Christmas observances take place.

In 1980, a circuit court of appeals ruled that schools in Sioux City, Iowa, could hold Christmas assemblies that included religious plays and songs. The court reasoned that the holiday observances had a "secular or cultural significance" and that "music, art, literature, and drama may be included in the curriculum...if presented in a prudent and objective manner and only as part of the cultural heritage of the holiday."[31] As of 1990, the U.S. Supreme Court had not decided any cases that dealt with the holiday observances in public schools.

To help schools decide about these matters, a pamphlet called *Religious Holidays in the Public Schools: Questions and Answers* was developed by representatives from sixteen religious and educational groups. The group offers guidelines for observing holidays in schools and using them as educational opportunities, saying that teachers can focus upon the "origin, history, and generally agreed-upon meaning of the observances. If the approach is objective, neither advancing nor inhibiting religion, it can foster among students understanding and mutual respect within and beyond the local community."[32] The key, according to this group and others, is respect—for different religious beliefs and for the constitutional guarantee of religious liberty.

RELIGION AND THE SCHOOL CURRICULUM

In 1859, Charles Darwin (1809–1882) published a book entitled *On The Origin of Species by Means of Natural Selection.* Darwin had traveled on a worldwide scientific expedition, studying fossils and living plants and animals. He had noticed links and similarities among various organisms, leading him to conclude that living things were not created separately but evolved gradually from common ancestry.

As Darwin's theory of evolution took hold in scientific circles, it also was much discussed by many nonscientists, including members and leaders of various religious denominations. Many Protestant churches discussed Darwin's theories, but the most conservative churches called evolution "heresy," a false and irreverent denial of the divine Creation of man as described in the Bible. They rejected the idea that humans had descended, or ascended, from a lower order of animals, namely apes. Some Protestant leaders wrote pamphlets urging people to interpret the story of Creation and other parts of the Bible literally.[1]

Interestingly, many other religious individuals

and groups found the theory of evolution compatible with their beliefs. Among these individuals were a good many scientists. One argument, still used today, was that regardless of the validity of Darwin's ideas, God still had created the mechanism of evolution. God made the dust out of which the first organisms arose, and God forged the process of evolution. Such ideas do not conflict with science, because they cannot be tested experimentally, so—at least according to these more liberal religious people—it is not a problem to believe in both evolution and God.

Clearly, debates about religion and the schools go beyond the matters of devotional exercises and holiday observances. People also disagree about what students should study when parts of the school curriculum conflict with their religious beliefs.

CONTROVERSIES OVER TEACHING EVOLUTION

By the 1900s, more children attended high school than ever before, because more schooling was required by law and was needed for many jobs. Some parents protested that school science books included Darwin's theory, which differed sharply from the account of Creation in the Old Testament Book of Genesis. The Bible says that God created various animals, then humans, separately, within six days. These citizens promoted laws to bar schools from teaching students about evolution. Between 1920 and 1926 eight southern states passed such laws. Elsewhere, some school boards told teachers not to present Darwin's ideas.

In 1925, after Tennessee passed a law forbidding the teaching of evolution theories in public schools, biology teacher John Thomas Scopes tested the law in Dayton, Tennessee. Clarence Darrow defended Scopes. Darrow was a famous trial lawyer known for helping disadvantaged clients, especially in cases involving civil liberties and academic freedom. Defending the state law was William Jennings Bryan, a noted orator and fundamentalist who believed in a literal reading of the Bible.

During the 1925 trial spectators and reporters crowded the hot courtroom to hear the two lawyers' impassioned arguments. In the end, Scopes was found guilty of breaking the state law that prohibited the teaching of evolutionary theory. He was fined one hundred dollars, but the state supreme court reversed the conviction on a technicality, so the case never reached the U.S. Supreme Court.

Forty years later, in December 1965, the city of Little Rock, Arkansas, found itself in the news. A twenty-four-year-old high school biology teacher named Susan Epperson challenged a state law that prohibited the teaching of evolution in Arkansas public schools. An Arkansas native, Epperson had chosen a new edition of a textbook called *Modern Biology* (an edition of which is still in print) for her tenth-grade classes. The book mentioned British scientist Charles Darwin and his theory of evolution. Because she had used a textbook that discussed Darwin's theories, Epperson faced fines and possible dismissal from her job.

The case of *Epperson v. Arkansas* did reach the U.S. Supreme Court. Epperson's attorney said that the Arkansas law violated both her right to free speech and the establishment clause of the First Amendment, which says that "Congress shall make no law respecting an establishment of religion." The Court agreed with Epperson, saying that a state cannot ban the teaching of a scientific theory because it conflicts with a particular religious viewpoint. Writing for a unanimous Court, Justice Abe

Fortas said that the First Amendment requires government to be neutral both in regard to various religions and between religion and nonreligion. He wrote, "The Arkansas law cannot be defended as an act of religious neutrality." He said it not only established a certain religious view but also prevented the free exercise of different views.[2]

Susan Epperson later said, "I was raised with the idea that you could certainly be a Christian, which both of my parents were, and still accept the evidence for evolution.... I'm a science teacher and if you've studied some science...you understand that evolution is a very unifying principle in the understanding of all kinds of biology. To leave it out, to not be able to say anything about it, is really shortchanging your students, not giving them the full picture."[3]

THE EVOLUTION CONTROVERSY TODAY

Despite the ruling in *Epperson*, the evolution controversy did not go away. In fact, in the years since, it has become increasingly heated, as school boards, state committees, legislatures, and publishers have argued about the propriety of teaching evolution in the schools. This battle has led to some interesting turnarounds. For example, evolution used to be taught in California; then it was forbidden in books and classes; now it has to be taught, and textbooks giving evolution short shrift are not adopted for classroom use. And as in the controversies over Bible reading and school prayer, the people who want evolution out of the schools and religion in the schools continue to look for ways to achieve their aims and stay within the law.

Evolution controversy now includes a debate over whether to teach creationism—the biblical story of the earth's creation—in addition to evolution. Those who advocate this view have developed materials that challenge the reasoning behind the different theories of evolution. For instance, creationism is now often called "creation science" in order to make it more acceptable in the eyes of the judicial and scientific establishment. Trained scientists who believe in creationism but not in evolution have joined this effort to attempt to scientifically prove the biblical account of the earth's creation and to disprove evolutionary theory.

David Muralt, of the fundamentalist Christian group Citizens for Excellence in Education, supports the idea of teaching creationism as a part of the public school curriculum. He says that to present only the theory of evolution "is discrimination and a grievous offense to the child that believes in creation."[4] Muralt and others think teachers should give equal time to each viewpoint. Needless to say, creation science has been intensely debated in different circles. Most scientists call creation science a pseudoscience, some of them quite vehemently.

The controversy has also reached the courts. In 1982, Arkansas adopted an equal-time law requiring teachers to present creationism along with the theory of evolution. The law was challenged in United States District Court by a group including ministers from different faiths and prominent scientists. The court overturned the law, saying that the view of human origins found in the Book of Genesis "has no scientific factual basis."[5]

A similar Louisiana law was struck down in 1987 by the U.S. Supreme Court. In *Edwards v. Aguillard*, seventy-two Nobel laureates said that creationism is not based upon scientific research; therefore, it does not meet the legal tests for "evidence." Justice William J. Brennan said that the

Louisiana law violated the establishment clause of the Constitution, because it had a clear purpose of advancing a specific religious viewpoint.[6]

Justices William H. Rehnquist and Antonin Scalia pointed out that teachers should be free to state that some religious groups disagree with the theory of evolution. Teachers may also present any available scientific data that support the creationism viewpoint as well as any scientific evidence that disputes evolution theories.[7]

In considering the various points of view, one must keep in mind that, strictly speaking, only assertions or ideas whose validity can be tested by experiment and/or whose *falsity* can be proved properly fall within the domain of science. Scientists cannot prove or disprove God's existence, so the existence of God is not something that scientists can study. This thinking was behind the statement by the Nobel laureates. Again, they and the courts were *not* saying God doesn't exist—indeed, at least some and probably many of the Nobel laureates and members of the Court do believe in God—only that they think that creationism, not being "based upon scientific research," should not be taught in the schools because of its religious basis.

CENSORSHIP OF BOOKS

Some people object on religious grounds to texts and library books besides those that discuss evolution. In 1989, a group of parents persuaded the staff of Boron High School, in California, to remove several books, including J. D. Salinger's *The Catcher in the Rye*, from the school's reading list. Commenting on this event, Anne Levinson, director of the Office of Intellectual Freedom in Chicago, said the action was "not unusual.... Censorship is still very much with us. I think *The Catcher in the Rye* is a perennial No. 1 on the censorship hit list."[8]

Ms. Levinson listed the reasons that parents object to certain books: "Usually the complaints have to do with blasphemy or what people feel is irreligious, or they say they find the language generally offensive or vulgar, or there is a sort of general 'family values' kind of complaint, that the book undermines parental authority, that the portrayal of Holden Caulfield is not a good role model for teenagers."[9]

A civil liberties group, People for the American Way, found that attacks on library books are increasing. In 1989 there were 172 parental protests nationwide, compared with 157 in 1988. Besides *The Catcher in the Rye*, schools have banned John Steinbeck's *The Grapes of Wrath* and *Of Mice and Men*, plays by Arthur Miller, Mark Twain's *The Adventures of Huckleberry Finn*, and Maya Angelou's *I Know Why the Caged Bird Sings*. Parents objected to profanity and sexual content in certain books.[10]

In 1985, members of a conservative church in Mobile, Alabama, joined other parents to protest a long list of books in the local schools. The parents said the books taught "secular humanism," which they defined as a religion that denies the existence of God, a supernatural Being or a Creator. They objected to secular humanism, saying that it gives a central role to human beings and their ideas rather than to biblical teachings and the commandments of God.

In *Smith v. Mobile County Board of School Commissioners*, a federal district court judge, W. Brevard Hand, agreed with the parents that secular humanism was a "godless" religion.[11] He ordered that forty-five books be removed from the schools.

Later that year, the U.S. Court of Appeals for the Eleventh Circuit overruled Judge Hand's decision, saying that the parents had not shown conclusively that the schools were promoting a religion. The parents did not appeal their case to the U.S. Supreme Court.

To many people who favor teaching evolution and oppose the teaching of creation science, Bible reading, and school prayer, the use of the secular-humanism argument seemed a ploy to get back at them. Trying to label secular humanism a religion seemed like fighting fire with fire. Creationists seemed to be saying, "If we can't get them to stop teaching evolution and let us teach religion, then we'll prove that evolution, liberalism, freethinking, and all the rest of it is also a religion, so it can't be taught."

PUTTING RELIGION BACK INTO THE SCHOOLS

While the high Court and many individuals seem bent on removing many of the influences of religion in the schools, a new trend has arisen that seems to put some religion *back* into the schools. Behind this trend are, oddly, some of the very same groups and individuals who want to keep religion out of the schools. How can this be?

These people, who include Americans United for Separation of Church and State, think classes such as social studies ought to give more attention to the role that religion has played in American life. They say that although school officials may not lead religious exercises, students should learn *about* religion. Although some students now learn about different religions and the role of religion in history, others do not, or spend little time on the subject. Supporters of adding material about religion to school curricula say that it can be combined with other subjects, such as history—for example, immigration, patterns of American settlement, the movement to abolish slavery. This teaching can be done, they say, without recommending a certain religious viewpoint. This movement, then, is not attempting to require students to practice religion but rather to study it and to investigate its role in American history and society.

There is also a growing effort to add material about religion to textbooks. Many textbook publishers, worried about controversy, have given the subject of religion little attention in their texts. People for the American Way examined thirty-one junior and senior high school history texts and concluded that they "treat religion by exclusion or by brief and simplistic reference. Honest treatment of religion in American history seems to be equated with advocacy of particular religious ideas and practices."[12] Among the neglected subjects, the group listed religious intolerance, religious idealism, and religion's role in social reform, the labor movement, politics, Prohibition, and antiwar debates. The group also said that books failed to discuss either conservative or liberal religious viewpoints: "left and right in the world of religion are ignored equally."[13]

Can religion be discussed in public schools so that no group feels it is being ignored or treated unfairly? In the 1963 *Abington* prayer and Bible reading case, Justice Tom Clark stressed the value of the "study of comparative religion [and] history of religion and its relationship to the advancement of civilization. It certainly may be said that the Bible is worthy of study for its literary and historic qualities. Nothing we have said here indicates that such study of the Bible or of religion, when presented objectively as part of a secular program of education, may not be effected consistently with the First Amendment."[14]

This crucifixion scene in a New York State public school
was at the heart of a recent controversy over separation of
church and state.

Bridget Mergens (center) won a Supreme Court decision that ruled that religious clubs may meet in public school buildings after regular school hours.

During the Inquisition, the Catholic church punished people who disagreed with its views, sometimes jailing, torturing, or killing them.

In 1742, New York City was home to many denominations.
From left to right, the churches are Lutheran, French,
Trinity, New Dutch, Old Dutch, Presbyterian, Baptist,
Quaker, and a synagogue.

In America, the Puritans were intolerant
of non-Puritans, especially Quakers, whom they
sometimes whipped, mutilated, or hanged.

A Quaker meeting in Philadelphia

A modern depiction of Jews worshipping during the eighteenth
century. During the Revolutionary War, several of
Philadelphia's leading citizens helped to construct Mikveh
Israel Synagogue. Later, the congregation of Mikveh Israel
donated land for a Protestant church.

The adoption of the Bill of Rights did not end religious
persecution by individuals or states. Here, Mormons are
shown being massacred in Missouri in 1838.

In the nineteenth century,
expanding U.S. borders
offered fresh territory for
settlement by members of
various religious groups,
including Mormons.

In *Abington School District* v. *Schempp*, the Supreme Court
ruled that Bible reading in public schools is unconstitutional.
The two defendants are shown here—Edward Schempp on the left
and his wife, third from the right.

Special periods for religious
instruction in public schools,
were ruled unconstitutional
by the Supreme Court in 1948.
Vashti McCollum, who went to
court in the name of her son,
is holding the newspaper
reporting the victory.

The Supreme Court has ruled that prayer in
public schools is unconstitutional, but many people still
question the decision.

One of the responses to
the Supreme Court's 1962
decision banning prayer
in public schools

Ishmael Jaffree (left), seen here with his lawyer, won a 1985 Supreme Court case involving school prayer. During the hearing, the plaintiff argued that silent prayer did not infringe on students' rights. In response, Justice Thurgood Marshall pointed out that students do not need legal permission to pray silently.

Some U.S schools have traditional pageants, songs, and decorations during religious holidays such as Christmas. These students are participating in a Christmas play.

In 1925, teacher John Scopes challenged a Tennessee law forbidding the teaching of the theory of evolution in public schools. The trial was called the Scopes Monkey trial.

In December 1965, biology teacher Susan Epperson challenged a state law banning the teaching of evolution in Arkansas public schools.

Around the country, various books have been banned as
a result of complaints from conservative religious groups.
These books include studies of the Holocaust, certain fairy
tales, and works by such classic American authors as
Hawthorne, Twain, and Steinbeck.

The Pawtucket, Rhode Island,
religious display that figured
in a 1984 Supreme Court decision.
The court ruled that public money
could be used to build the display.

Crowds of shoppers on a Sunday in the famous Orchard
Street bargain-shopping district in New York City.
The many stores owned by Orthodox Jews are
closed on Saturdays and open on Sundays. Do you
think that closing these stores on Sundays
would serve a good purpose?

Some Native Americans use peyote, a cactus that contains a hallucinatory drug, in certain religious ceremonies.

Members of some religious groups, such as the followers of the Reverend Sun Myung Moon, have claimed religious persecution by communities and by the government. In 1982, he presided over a mass wedding of 2,200 couples. In many nontraditional religious groups or cults, all marriages must be approved by the leader.

Saluting the flag in 1957

Many Americans approve of the idea of an official
moment of silence for students beginning the day
in public schools. The question remains, is this moment
of silence really a moment of prayer in disguise?
And is the spirit embodied in the American flag
really served best by such a practice?

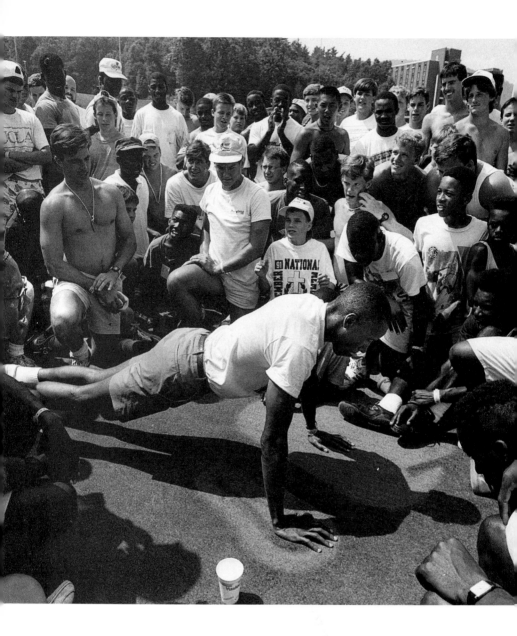

Nearly 10,000 student athletes, coaches, and their families
attend over sixty-five Fellowship of Christian Athletes
camps around the country every summer where "inspiration
and perspiration" are joined together. Such organizations
would like to expand their presence in the schools.

Students might discuss Native American religions, colonists and other immigrants who sought religious liberty in America, communities based on religious values, comparative religion, religious prejudice, interfaith cooperation, and the contributions that America's religious groups have made to social reform. Studies about religion, with exposure to different viewpoints, would differ from devotionals or the promotion of one creed. Albert Shanker, president of the American Federation of Teachers, is among those who say such courses could enhance students' understanding of history and culture in America and other lands.

FUTURE DIRECTIONS

For many Americans, the questions about separation of church and state in the schools are the most crucial of all. The 1962 and 1963 decisions to prohibit official school prayers and Bible reading challenged heartfelt beliefs about how young people should be taught and reared. The decisions ended long-standing traditions and occurred at a stressful time in American life, when a controversial war was being fought in Vietnam and other traditional morals and values were being challenged.

Some Americans worry that contemporary social problems—a loss of discipline, rising rates of teenage pregnancy, high divorce rates, crime and violence, drug and alcohol abuse—are linked to a decrease in religious symbols and practices. Among those who hold this viewpoint are the Reverend Mr. Jerry Falwell, leader of the Moral Majority, a group that urges a return to traditional values and school prayer, and Beverly La Haye, head of Concerned Women for America. Their opponents say that today's social problems are complex and that the absence of school prayer and other public religious expressions is not the cause.

Can some common ground between these arguing groups be found? Speaking about the role of religion in schools, Oliver Thomas, spokesperson for the Baptist Joint Committee on Public Affairs, expressed optimism. Thomas addressed a news conference at which educators and religious leaders discussed booklets they had written to help public schools make decisions about religious issues, such as celebrating holidays in the schools. Noting that the group represented a "broad spectrum" of religions and educational viewpoints, Thomas said that their work together showed "that questions concerning religion in the public schools do have answers that capture a common vision for the common good."[15]

C H A P T E R

7

PUBLIC AID
FOR RELIGIOUS INSTITUTIONS
AND ACTIVITIES

Michelle, a ninth grader at a Catholic school, does not pay to ride on the school bus. Some of her schoolbooks are bought with public taxes. Bus transportation and nonreligious textbooks are two examples of aid to religious schools allowed by the courts. States may also provide materials that parochial schools need to give state-ordered tests of basic skills. As a result of a 1965 federal aid-to-education law, states can decide how to distribute certain federal education funds, and it is legitimate to give some of this money to religious schools.

Needless to say, "legitimate" does not equal "noncontroversial," and like other issues involving church and state, the one involving public aid for religious schools is nothing if not controversial.

When James Madison protested the use of taxes to support religious organizations in 1775, government was much simpler than it is today. Now there are far more public institutions and a greater dependence on government funding. Over the years, government has found ways to support religion both directly and indirectly—including directing some money toward parochial schools. Other recipients of public aid or tax breaks include religious organizations. Local governments sometimes use tax money to set up religious displays during holidays. Can government money ever be used to aid religion? Or does any public aid to a religious group breach the wall of separation between church and state?

TAX EXEMPTIONS FOR RELIGIOUS ORGANIZATIONS

In all fifty states, religious organizations receive property tax exemptions. In other words, churches, synagogues, mosques, and other places of worship do not pay local property taxes. The Supreme Court has said that the First Amendment does not prevent state and local governments from taxing religious property, yet communities grant religious organizations this privilege. Community leaders and citizens have reasoned that religious groups, along with other charitable and nonprofit groups, such as the United Way, benefit the community. They run charitable programs, such as food banks, and offer recreational and educational activities for people in the community.

In 1970, in *Walz v. Tax Commission*, the U.S. Supreme Court had to decide if a New York law exempting places of worship from taxation was constitutional. Writing for the majority, Chief Justice Warren Burger said that such laws may be constitutional. He called this type of impartial aid to religion a "benevolent neutrality"—that is, aid which benefits all nonprofit organizations the same way. The Court said that while examining the New York law, they had concluded that the tax advantages applied equally to all houses of worship, along with other nonprofit organizations—hospitals, libraries, playgrounds, and historical and patriot groups.[1]

Not taxing religious organizations has several results. From a practical standpoint, such taxation might increase government entanglement with religion. The state would have to assess taxes and initiate legal processes such as tax liens and foreclosures. Tax exemptions also help smaller, less affluent religious groups to survive.

TAXING RELIGIOUS ORGANIZATIONS

Religious organizations are required to pay taxes on certain commercial activities. A church that runs a for-profit venture, such as making and selling pottery or clothing, is taxed like other businesses. A failure to impose such taxes would force similar businesses to compete with a business that could keep prices low and still make a profit. On the other hand, these businesses, whether for-profit or nonprofit, do contribute earnings for work that benefits the community.

Even the sale of religious books is taxed. In a case involving the television evangelist Jimmy Swaggart, the state of California insisted that he pay taxes on profits from books and tapes that his organization sold in that state. When the U.S. Supreme Court ruled on the case, Justice Sandra Day O'Connor explained that taxes on commercial ventures are not aimed at the right to express religious information, ideas, or beliefs, but such taxes may be imposed when profits are made by selling "tangible personal property."[2]

PUBLIC AID FOR RELIGIOUS SCHOOLS

Recently, debates are intensifying about the use of taxes to help support private religious schools—also called sectarian or parochial schools. About 12 percent of U.S. children are enrolled in such schools.

Three out of five private school students attend Roman Catholic schools; the others attend nonsectarian private schools or those operated by other faiths, including Jewish, Lutheran, and Seventh-Day Adventist.[3]

For more than a century, advocates of parochial schools have argued that these schools should get the same tax support as public schools. Catholic schools in particular have faced increasing financial problems since the 1960s. Fewer people have been joining religious orders of nuns, brothers, and priests, so laypeople—those not belonging to religious orders—must be hired at higher costs. Also, parochial schools in urban areas have faced lower enrollments as more families moved to the suburbs. Aging school buildings need repairs, but less money has been available to fix and maintain them. Inflation and rising costs have compounded these problems.

In response, some states have devised plans to aid parochial schools. The courts have judged what kinds of aid to religious schools violate separation of church and state. Some justices have opposed all kinds of aid, saying that the wall between church and state should be high and rigid. Other justices have taken the position that aid is permissible, because church and state must work together to achieve many goals, such as educating children to become good citizens. In trying to reconcile different viewpoints, the Supreme Court has adopted guidelines to judge whether certain types of aid can be given to religious schools: (1) the purpose must be secular (nonreligious), not sectarian; (2) the primary effect must be neither to enhance nor to hinder religion; (3) there must be no excessive entanglement between church and state.[4]

Some innovative plans that have gained support in recent years would aid all private schools, religious or not. Allowing parents to deduct private school tuition from their taxable income each year is one way that government helps with the cost of such schooling. One plan would give parents educational vouchers—coupons redeemable for tuition to attend any public or private school approved by the state board of education. The idea of school choice has been supported by President George Bush and others who claim that it would improve America's education system. Supporters of vouchers and school choice plans say that if people can choose any school they want, schools will become more competitive, improving quality.

Catholic school advocates think that voucher and choice plans would remove the financial barriers that prevent some parents from sending their children to parochial schools. The church has organized groups to represent Catholic parents on legislative matters and to tell them about bills before Congress or state legislatures that affect freedom of choice in education.[5] Concerns about this issue run deep, especially because almost every school, parochial or public, can use more funding.

AID FOR RELIGIOUS SCHOOLS: PRO

In addition to having the authority to allocate public funds to parochial schools for transportation, nonreligious textbooks, and materials for testing, states may permit parents to deduct from their state income taxes a given amount for tuition, books, and transportation paid for private schooling, including sectarian education. In one case, the Supreme Court let a state provide such deductions because parents of public school children took deductions for some of their expenses, too, although their expenses were much lower. The Court reasoned that private schools reduce the taxes for all citizens.

Supporters of aid to parochial schools say that even if such aid benefits religion in minor ways, that does not matter. The government wants to educate each child, and children can receive a basic education in either a public or a religious school. Supporters also say that children and their parents should have the right to choose any licensed school. If a lack of money prevents them from choosing a parochial school, they are denied the free exercise of their beliefs. Catholic parents have said that when they send their children to parochial schools, they face double taxation. They must pay for both public education and the parochial school.

Supporters say that parochial schools benefit society. Leonard Levy, a constitutional law expert, writes that these schools reduce "the tax burden for the operation of the public schools." Private funds build the schools, and most of the operating costs come from private sources and parents, who also pay taxes for public schools. Levy adds, "Good education in an environment marked by better discipline, less violence, crime, and drugs, and better attendance records also speaks well for religious schools."[6] Other supporters cite studies showing that parochial schools educate economically disadvantaged students better than public schools do.[7]

AID FOR RELIGIOUS SCHOOLS: CON

Aid that is usually forbidden by the courts is that which goes straight to parochial schools themselves, such as teacher salaries and tuition payments.[8] Yet strict church-state separationists say that *any* aid violates the constitutional ban on an establishment of religion. They say that parochial schools are clearly religious institutions with a primary goal of teaching religion. Tax money—which comes from the whole population—should not be given to such schools, say critics such as John Swomley, a well-known writer on church-state issues.

Opponents of public aid for parochial schools find quotes from the nation's Founding Fathers to support their views: "When a religion is good, I conceive it will support itself," said Benjamin Franklin.[9] "It is sinful and tyrannical to compel a man to furnish contributions for the propagation of opinions which he disbelieves...it is also wrong to force him to support this or that teacher of his own religious persuasion," said Thomas Jefferson.[10] They also cite James Madison's *Remonstrance* against Virginia's plan to support religious teachers.

People who oppose aid for parochial schools argue that private education is a privilege, not a right. Private schools can choose whom to admit and keep, but public schools must serve everyone. Aid to private schools makes less money available for public education. It gives unfair benefits to the Catholic church, which operates most parochial schools, say critics.

RELIGIOUS DISPLAYS ON PUBLIC PROPERTY

Another issue involving government support of religion is the use of taxes and public property for religious displays, especially during holiday seasons. Displays of Christian nativity scenes (mangers or crèches—scenes with the infant Jesus) and Jewish menorahs (a menorah is a candelabrum displayed in celebration of the Jewish eight-day holiday of Hanukkah, celebrated the same month as Christmas) on town-owned property have fueled debates in recent years.

In 1984, the Supreme Court ruled in *Lynch v. Donnelly* that Pawtucket, Rhode Island, could use city tax money to build a holiday display that included a religious symbol—the crèche. The display was placed on private property, and the city joined with local merchants to fund the scene, part of a larger holiday display that included nonreligious symbols. The opinion, written by Chief Justice Warren Burger, expressed an accommodationist viewpoint—the idea that government can work with religious organizations in certain ways. Burger said that the Constitution does not require "complete separation of church and state [but] affirmatively mandates accommodation, not merely tolerance, of all religions, and forbids hostility toward any."[11]

Justice Burger cited an "unbroken history of official acknowledgment by all three branches of government of the role of religion in American life"—the proclamation of Thanksgiving as a national holiday, the motto "In God we trust," and the use of religious slogans in various settings.[12] He said that Christmas has long been recognized as a national holiday. Burger acknowledged also that the Court had once ruled the Ten Commandments cannot be posted in public schools, because that might appear to be a "religious admonition." Yet, he said, a crèche can be seen in the context of the holiday season, not as a hidden effort to express government support "of a particular religious message."[13]

Rob Boston, an editor for the pro-separation magazine *Church & State*, believes that "Christmas in America is an unusual mixture of the secular and the sacred. Communities across the country bear witness to this fact each year with holiday displays that run the gamut: Frosty the Snowman and Santa Claus alongside the Baby Jesus and a manger scene; Mary and Joseph paired with dancing elves beneath a Christmas tree."[14]

Since the Pawtucket, Rhode Island, case, some communities have been confused by the Court's ruling. Many are unwilling to end traditional displays on public property. In 1989 the Supreme Court heard the case of *Allegheny County v. American Civil Liberties Union, Greater Pittsburgh Chapter*. Citizens in Pittsburgh, Pennsylvania, including a Muslim, a Unitarian, and several Jews, objected to a manger placed in front of the Allegheny County courthouse. The Court ruled that the Nativity scene could not be displayed alone, but must be combined with other nonreligious "seasonal" symbols.[15]

In a related decision, the Court said that a menorah was allowed because it stood beside a Christmas tree in a public park.[16] It was therefore part of a general holiday incorporating both Christmas and Hanukkah as part of "the same winter-holiday season, which has attained a secular status in our society."[17] The American Civil Liberties Union and some others who advocate strict separation of church and state had urged the Court to ban all religious displays on public property. Different Jewish groups and Christian denominations were split among themselves, some supporting and others opposing the decision.

Some clergy maintain that it is not necessary or desirable to remove religious symbols from public property. Other clergy point out that churches and synagogues may still sponsor religious displays, even if public places do not. Robert L. Maddox of Americans United for the Separation of Church and State, says, "In a religiously diverse population like ours that cherishes religious freedom, such symbols are best displayed on private property."[18] The Holy Name Society of Pittsburgh, owner of the crèche at issue in the Court decision, has decided to display it on private property rather than surround this deeply religious symbol with nonreligious items.

In response to the 1989 Pittsburgh decision, the *Detroit Free Press* said that, "crèches and menorahs are vital symbols of faith in God—when they are displayed, proudly and reverently, in houses of worship and private homes, not cheapened by bland celebrations at government buildings."[19] *The Los Angeles Times* wrote that using "religious symbols for a purely secular purpose—be it political or commercial—is and should be offensive to sincere believers.... [It] is an open invitation to endless and needlessly divisive legislation."[20]

Maddox writes that the Supreme Court decision in the Rhode Island (*Lynch*) case "leaves considerable confusion about the use of public property by religious groups, especially the government's role in supporting such use."[21] The Court has said that religious symbols may be displayed on public property if they are combined with nonreligious symbols. Those religious organizations that agree with the editorials above may decide not to place religious displays on public property along with secular (nonreligious) symbols. The lingering confusion about religious displays on public property may result in new court cases as people try to clarify these issues.

C H A P T E R

8

CONFLICTS OVER THE FREE EXERCISE OF RELIGION

During the nineteenth century the courts dealt with the subject of plural marriage—marriage to more than one person—as practiced by some Mormons, members of the Church of Jesus Christ of Latter-day Saints. At that time, the practice of plural marriage was a part of the Mormon faith, but U.S. laws forbade marriage to more than one person at the same time. In 1879, the Supreme Court ruled in *Reynolds v. United States* that separation of church and state did not forbid Congress from passing laws needed for the common good. The Court said the laws against bigamy were constitutional even if they interfered with free exercise of religion, because society has the right to maintain laws protecting the institution of marriage, which the justices called basic to Western civilization.[1]

Two other 1890 rulings, *Davis v. Beason* and *In re: Church of Jesus Christ of Latter-day Saints*, were later criticized as unfair. In *Davis*, the Court upheld laws that denied Mormons voting rights.[2] In the second case, it allowed state governments to seize property held by the Mormon church, except

---

buildings used solely for worship.³ Mormons were persecuted and driven from several states. These conflicts subsided in 1897 after the church abandoned the practice of plural marriage.

Just as the Constitution forbids laws "respecting an establishment of religion"—exemplified by many of the cases discussed in earlier chapters—so it forbids laws that hinder "the free exercise" of religion. In cases such as *Reynolds*, however, the Court has balanced the right to free exercise against other factors and has wound up limiting free exercise. What does free exercise mean in practical, everyday terms? Can people do whatever they wish in the name of religion? Can they disobey a law? Can they endanger other people? A number of issues, each seemingly of a different nature, are actually related to one another through the thread of free exercise.

BALANCING GOVERNMENT ACTIONS AND FREE EXERCISE OF RELIGION

Since the 1950s, many cases regarding free exercise of religion have arisen because people, usually members of minority religious groups, find a law to be in conflict with their religious practices. How do courts decide whether government has taken an action that hinders the free exercise of religion?

The Supreme Court often uses a two-part test to balance the competing interests of the government and individuals. This test came from a 1963 case, *Sherbert v. Verner*. The Court held that a person cannot be denied the benefits of a public program because of the free exercise of religion, including observing Saturday as the Sabbath, a practice followed by Jews and several other religious groups in America.

Adell Sherbert, a member of the Seventh-Day

Adventist church, had been fired because she would not work on Saturday, her Sabbath. After she was fired, South Carolina officials denied her employee compensation (unemployment) benefits. The Court decided that this law put an unnecessary burden on Adell Sherbert's free exercise of religion, because no "compelling state interest" was served by restricting Sherbert's First Amendment rights. The Court said that a two-part test would apply in such cases: First, the government must show that an important public policy, such as health or safety concerns, was at stake. After showing such a reason, the government must then prove that it could not have achieved its goal with less restrictive alternatives.[4]

CONSCIENTIOUS OBJECTION TO MILITARY SERVICE

A major church-state issue that is literally a matter of life or death involves conscientious objectors—people who object to bearing arms, taking part in war, and participating in military training and activities. Throughout human history, peace has been rare. According to one source, since documented history began, the world has been at peace only about 8 percent of the time—or 286 out of the past 3,550 years.[5] At the same time, "thou shalt not kill" has been a widely accepted religious concept since biblical times. In 1948 the World Council of Churches stated, "War is contrary to the will of God."

From colonial days, some Americans, often members of pacifist churches, have refused to fight in wars. The Society of Friends (Quakers) said in 1660: "We utterly deny all outward wars and strife and fightings with outward weapons, for any end or under any pretense whatever, and we do certainly know, and do testify to the world, that the spirit of Christ, which leads us into all truth, will never move us to fight and war against any man with outward weapons, neither for the kingdom of God nor for the kingdom of this world."⁶

In 1775, Anthony Benezet, a Quaker, called war "premeditated and determined destruction of human beings, creatures fashioned after the image of God."⁷ He told Christians to refuse to fight or pay military taxes and to urge the government not to go to war. About 50,000 Quakers lived in the Colonies in 1776 when the Revolutionary War began. Their teachings opposed military service, militia drills, and the taking of oaths. Many Quakers were imprisoned, beaten, and sentenced to hard labor after refusing to do these things.

Other sects, guided by the pacifist beliefs of the early Christians, also objected to military service. These groups included Mennonites, Brethren, Moravians, Amish, Schwenckfelders, and a small group called Rogerenes in New England. During the Revolution, most pacifists took a neutral position. Some did war-related work, helping the wounded and other people who suffered from the war. Congress declared that religious objectors might give "relief to their distressed Brethren in the several Colonies, and [offer] other service to their oppressed country which they can, consistently with their Religious Principles."⁸ Yet some colonies punished objectors, so about 60,000 moved to Canada. Those who stayed faced fines, prison, or the loss of belongings—houses, barns, farm tools, and livestock.⁹

In 1789, James Madison urged the adoption of an amendment to the Constitution that would protect conscientious objectors, but it was not passed. Conscientious objectors faced the same problems during the War of 1812 and the Civil War. Men drafted for military service in the Civil War had the option of hiring or finding a substitute soldier to serve in their place. After the Civil War, men unwilling to bear arms had the option of doing some type of alternative service.

After the Supreme Court ruled the draft itself constitutional,[10] Congress assumed the task of writing a bill to protect conscientious objectors (COs). The Selective Service Act of 1917 gave specific exemptions to ordained ministers, students preparing for the ministry, and members of recognized "peace churches"—for example, Quakers, Amish, and Mennonites—whose creeds ban participation in war. Objectors could perform alternative service— for example, in military hospitals. However, these exemptions did not apply to non-church-affiliated objectors.

During World War II, *individual* religious conviction became the test for CO status. The Roosevelt administration changed the definition of COs to include any person, not necessarily belonging to a peace church, whose objections to war were based on religious training and belief in a Supreme Being.[11]

During the Vietnam War, the U.S. Supreme Court again enlarged the basis for exemption. The 1965 Draft Act cases—*United States v. Seeger*— involved three young men who did not have a traditionally based belief in God. One of the claimants, Daniel Seeger, said he had an open mind as to "belief in a Supreme Being." All three men said they had pacifist beliefs stemming from their sense of morality and ethics in human relationships. The Court unanimously granted these men the same exemption given to pacifists who base their ideas on traditional religious beliefs. The men had "a sincere and meaningful belief, which occupies in the life of its possessor a place parallel to that filled by the God" in the lives of other people, said the Court.[12]

In his book *The Right of the People*, Justice William O. Douglas explained the reasoning that led to this decision: "The First Amendment is not concerned with dogma alone, but with the conscience.... [When] the conscience of man cries out against taking a certain step or performing a certain act, he should have the same protection under the First Amendment as those whose conscientious objections have been formalized into a creed."[13]

The laws now recognize conscientious objection based either on a religious creed or on personal ethics, but the Supreme Court set a limit in 1970 when it ruled that a conscientious objector must oppose all wars, not just a specific war. The draft ended in 1973, but the 1980 renewal of Selective Service registration revived the issue of conscientious objection. During the 1991 war against Iraq, some members of army reserve units opposed the war and refused to go into combat, saying it was against their beliefs. Their critics asked why they had joined the reserves in the first place. Their cases are pending, and people are waiting to see if the courts will expand previous rulings on conscientious objection.

THE FLAG-SALUTE CASES

Patriotism, religion, and the Constitution intersect not only in the military but in the schools as well. On November 5, 1935, a ten-year-old in Minersville, Pennsylvania, wrote a letter to the directors of his school. The letter said, in part: "Dear Sirs, I do not salute the flag because I have promised to do the will of God. That means that I must not worship anything out of harmony with God's law. In the twentieth chapter of Exodus it is stated, 'Thou shalt not make unto thee any graven image nor bow down to them nor serve them....' I do not salute the flag because I do not love my country but I love my country and I love God more and I must abide by His commandments. Your pupil, Billy Gobitas."[14]

William and his sister Lillian, age twelve, had been expelled from school because they refused to take part in a required morning exercise including the Pledge of Allegiance and salute to the flag. As members of the Jehovah's Witnesses, a religious group sometimes criticized for its vigorous preaching, they were following their religious convictions. The question was, were they also being prevented by government from the free exercise of religion, as guaranteed by the Constitution?

During the 1930s, about two thousand children were expelled in thirty-one states because they refused to salute the flag.[15] Some state officials decided these children were delinquent and removed them from their parents' custody. Jehovah's Witnesses and their churches were attacked in hundreds of violent incidents. The mood of the nation was tense during the 1930s. Adolf Hitler and his German army were gaining power in Europe, and people worried about national security. To foster patriotism and unity, school officials in eighteen states and in hundreds of school districts required children to salute the flag each morning. Not everyone thought this was a good idea. A 1935 editorial in the *Baltimore Evening Sun* said, "Any statute requiring that the flag be saluted by school children is an insult to the Stars and Stripes.... Since when has the Star-Spangled Banner so lost the respect of the people over whom it flies that laws are necessary to make them pretend to honor it?"[16]

In Nazi Germany, Jehovah's Witnesses refused to join the compulsory flag salutes and raised-palm

Fascist salutes demanded by Hitler. Some were deported or sent to labor camps. In America, the Witnesses' leader, Joseph F. Rutherford, denounced all mandatory salutes, supporting his views with quotations from the Bible. Agreeing with their church leaders, William and Lillian Gobitas refused to salute the flag and were expelled from school.

Their father, Walter Gobitas, sued the school board. The board refused to readmit the children, so he sought help in federal district court and won. The school board appealed, and the U.S. Supreme Court agreed to hear the case. In court, Gobitas claimed that the Minersville school board had violated his children's First Amendment rights to free exercise of religion. In reply, the school board said that mandatory flag salutes promoted respect for flag and country. With war threatening, patriotism and loyalty were touchy issues.

In 1940, the Court ruled in favor of the school board. Justice Felix Frankfurter said that the case had been difficult to decide, but that the Gobitas family's religious beliefs were subject to the need to promote national unity.[17] One Justice, Harlan Fiske Stone, dissented. While endorsing the value of patriotism, Stone said that it should not override anyone's sincere belief in "the higher commandments of God" and that fostering patriotism should not deny people the freedoms for which America stands. Stone pointed out that a political minority like the Jehovah's Witnesses would probably not get help from the lawmakers. Speaking of the individual rights guarded by the Constitution, Stone said: "The very essence of the liberty which they [the 1st and 14th Amendments] guarantee is the freedom of the individual from compulsion as to what he shall think and what he shall say, at least where the compulsion is to bear false witness to his religion."[18]

After this 1940 decision, there were numerous attacks on Jehovah's Witnesses. Mobs disrupted Bible meetings and burned down Kingdom Halls in Maine and other states. Witnesses were insulted and beaten. They received malicious letters and were shunned by coworkers and former friends. In one West Virginia town, a mob, including the sheriff, kidnapped nine male Witnesses. The mob paraded its victims along the streets after forcing them to drink overdoses of castor oil, a strong laxative that can cause severe cramps and even internal bleeding.[19] Legal scholars, newspaper editors, and citizens, including First Lady Eleanor Roosevelt, criticized the decision in *Minersville School District v. Gobitis* [sic]. Clergymen of the Catholic church and other faiths also spoke out on behalf of the Witnesses.

Three years later the Supreme Court considered another flag-salute case involving seven West Virginia children. In 1943 the Court struck down mandatory flag-salute laws, thus reversing the *Gobitis* [sic] decision. The Court said that patriotism is best encouraged through persuasion and example, not forced tributes. The opinion in *West Virginia State Board of Education v. Barnette,* written by Justice Robert H. Jackson, is often quoted in First Amendment cases: "Those who begin coercive elimination of dissent soon find themselves exterminating dissenters. Compulsory unification of opinion achieves only the unanimity of the graveyard.... The First Amendment to our Constitution was designed to avoid these endings by avoiding these beginnings.... No official, high or petty, can prescribe what shall be orthodox in politics, nationalism, religion, or other matters of opinion or force citizens to confess by word or act, their faith therein. If there are any circumstances which permit an exception, they do not occur to us now."[20]

In 1985, Lillian Gobitas wrote about the problems she faced at age twelve when she took an unpopular stand in order to follow her religion: "I loved school, and I was with a nice group.... I was class president in the seventh grade, and I had good grades. And I felt that, Oh, if I stop saluting the flag, I will blow all this! And I did. It sure worked out that way."[21] One of Lillian's teachers praised her courage, but her classmates ostracized her and her former school never readmitted her. Even so, she says, "I would do it again in a second.... Jehovah's Witnesses are now banned in over forty countries. So we really try to build up our faith."[22]

COMPULSORY EDUCATION AND RELIGION

In 1972, some Amish parents in Wisconsin challenged laws that they found to be in conflict with their free exercise of religion. Mandatory education laws in most states, including Wisconsin, require children to attend school until age sixteen. Members of the Amish church follow a traditional farming way of life separate from the larger community. Families meet their own basic needs and help other community members, without government aid or modern conveniences such as telephones and electricity.

In *State of Wisconsin v. Jonas Yoder*, Amish parents said that forcing their children to attend school past the eighth grade hindered their religious practices and community life. They wanted their children to gain only basic skills needed for farming and such trades as carpentry. The Supreme Court ruled that the state could not force Amish parents to send their children to school beyond the eighth grade. The Court agreed that this state policy infringed upon sincere religious beliefs. It noted that the Amish give their children vocational training and teach them to become productive citizens in their community. Such preparation is an acceptable alternative to high school, said the Court.[23]

MEDICAL TREATMENT AND RELIGION

Can people refuse health care that goes against their religious beliefs? The courts have usually supported an adult's right to refuse such treatment, even if his or her life is at risk.

The Massachusetts Supreme Court tackled this problem in 1991 in *Norwood Hospital v. Muñoz*. A hospital sued a Jehovah's Witness who refused to accept blood transfusions to treat bleeding ulcers. Witnesses interpret the Bible to mean that they must not ingest blood. The court unanimously ruled that even when religious beliefs seem unwise to others, an adult has the right to "bodily integrity and privacy." [24] However, the courts have limited the free exercise of religion when other persons—a minor child or the general public—are at risk. In 1952, in *People ex rel. Wallace v. Labrenz*, the U.S. Supreme Court said that a state may require vaccinations to keep the public from being exposed to communicable diseases. The Court has also allowed blood transfusions and other treatments to save a child's life, even when the parents object on religious grounds.[25]

During the 1980s, some children of Christian Science families died after their parents relied upon spiritual rather than medical care. The parents were ordered to stand trial for manslaughter— causing the death of another without malice or intent. In a Massachusetts case, the parents were convicted. Their attorney had argued that Christian Scientists call a doctor only if they have a "crisis of faith."[26] The state argued that the parents had a duty to get lifesaving treatment for a minor child, in this case a two-and-a-half-year-old boy, who was too young to seek treatment on his own. After convicting the parents, the state put them on probation and ordered them to provide standard medical care for their three remaining children.

Founded in 1879, the Christian Scientist church has members called practitioners who are trained to use prayer and faith in God as a means of healing the sick. These practices are based on the belief that healing comes from God. The church also says that in many cases, documented by medical experts, spiritual healing has cured illnesses. In 1990 a church spokesman said, "We have never asked for the right to neglect children. We have asked for the right to practice spiritual healing. That for us is what the free exercise of religion is all about."[27]

What standards should be set in this area of law? Some people insist that a child's well-being must take priority over a parent's free exercise of religion. They say that laws should require all parents to get standard health care for their minor children. In these cases the well-being and even the lives of children may be at stake, along with the sincere religious beliefs of the parents, so they are troubling issues for the courts and for society.

FREE EXERCISE AND NATIVE AMERICANS

Several important church-state questions involve Native Americans. From colonial times, U.S. government policies have aimed to suppress traditional Indian religions. Early settlers thought they should convert Indians to Christian religions.

During the 1800s, Catholic and Protestant churches set up missions near Indian lands and urged them to change their religion. After the Indians were defeated and confined to reservations in the late 1800s, their children were sent to boarding schools where, again, they were taught the culture and religion of whites. During the 1900s, Native Americans asserted their right to follow traditional religions and customs and to help run their own schools.

In 1978, the American Indian Religious Freedom Act was signed into law. The act was intended to "protect and preserve the inherent right of American Indian, Eskimo, Aleut, and Native Hawaiian people to believe, express, and exercise their traditional religions."[28] It pledges to protect Indian access to cemeteries, sacred objects, and land used in religious rites.

Tribes have protested for years because archaeologists and others have dug up Indian skeletons—a practice that Indians consider sacrilegious. Moonface Bear of the Paugussett tribe in Connecticut said, "For so many years, the bones of our dead were treated like dinosaur bones—on display. They were dug up and put in a museum. Why our grounds? Not only has a living culture been taken away, but respect for the dead."[29] Indians are fighting to protect old burial sites containing ancestral bones and sacred objects. They have demanded the return of bones and objects that can be traced to particular tribes, and they are trying to reach an agreement with the Smithsonian Institution as well as with smaller, regional museums.

Another conflict has raged over the ceremonial use of peyote, a substance that comes from a small spineless cactus. Since about A.D. 200, certain tribes have used peyote during religious rites. About 200,000 members of the Native American Church, established over one hundred years ago, use it today during prayers. They also think that peyote has curative effects. However, in a 1990 case, *Employment Division v. Smith*, the Supreme Court ruled 6–3, that an Oregon law banning the use of peyote was constitutional. It said that the free exercise clause of the First Amendment does not exempt Native Americans from a "neutral, generally applicable law."[30]

Widespread concern about illegal drugs may have influenced the Court's decision in this case. State officials claimed that allowing religious exceptions for peyote use would weaken the government's ability to cope with the drug problem. They also argued that peyote may be harmful. Critics of the decision say that peyote use is a long-standing religious practice, comparable to other churches' use of wine. According to anthropologist Omer C. Steward, "Peyote is the essential ingredient of the Native American Church.... The church is based on the use of peyote as a sacrament."[31] Twenty-three states exempt Native Americans from laws banning peyote. The California Supreme Court has ruled that Native Americans may use peyote in rituals, saying that small quantities are unlikely to cause harm.[32] Texas regulates peyote distribution by keeping records of its disbursement and limiting its use to those who are at least one-quarter Indian.[33] The case of peyote is another example of the courts' willingness to set some limits on the free exercise of religion. This time, however, the Supreme Court has merely upheld the states' rights to apply some limitations if they *choose* to.

CULT MOVEMENTS

Americans were shocked in 1978 to hear about a tragedy in Guyana: 911 members of the People's

Temple, along with their leader, Jim Jones, had committed suicide or been forced to die by drinking cyanide. Jones had inspired his followers with sermons about a better world, free of racism and poverty, before he led them to the remote jungle where they died.

The People's Temple is regarded as a cult, in contrast to traditional or other Creator-centered religions. Cults are often defined as religious groups with forceful leaders who expect unquestioning trust and obedience. Some cults require members to give their possessions and income to the organization.

Many new cults have formed in the United States since the early 1960s. In 1984, it was estimated that from several hundred thousand to three million Americans belonged to cults.[34] One large, well-known cult is Korean-born Sun Myung Moon's Unification Church, whose members are known as Moonies. Critics say that this cult alienates members from their families and brainwashes them. Parents of young people in the cult have kidnapped their children and hired professionals to "deprogram" them, to rid their minds of cult philosophy. Other groups that have been called cults include the Worldwide Church of God, the International Society for Krishna Consciousness (better known as Hare Krishnas), and the Divine Light Mission of Guru Maharaj Ji.

The deaths in Guyana and concern about the recruiting and money-raising ventures of cults have led to government investigations of cult activities. Tax laws and those that apply to public health and welfare are used to regulate some of their activities. Sun Myung Moon and other leaders have been accused of failing to pay taxes on business profits. Some cults, such as the Hare Krishnas, have been investigated for violating labor laws; others have been convicted of child abuse after they beat children as punishment. The Church of Scientology was involved in a long legal battle over business matters.

In many of these cases, cult members have complained that because they were nontraditional and sometimes unpopular, the government was systematically trying to destroy them, totally taking away their free exercise of religion. One could argue that when more traditional churches show signs of dubious business practices, they are not investigated with such fervor. On the other hand, in recent years—as is witnessed by many of the cases discussed in this book and by other cases, such as the one involving Jim and Tammy Bakker—the government appears to be vigilant with traditional religions as well. Indeed, some of the Fundamentalist Christian churches—especially those led by television evangelists—are accorded treatment similar to that given to the cults.

Yet clergymen from mainstream churches say that problems can arise for all religions if government undertakes special investigations of unpopular religious movements. Regulations that affect one may affect all. In a 1990 book, *Leaving Cults: The Dynamics of Defection*, Stuart A. Wright argues that cults have a high turnover rate, with 95 to 99 percent of the members leaving on their own. He said that most cult influence resembles that used in advertising, peer pressure, and other types of persuasion in society. Wright concludes that "there's a double standard operating here. They're picking on these groups because they don't like them."[35]

OTHER PUBLIC POLICY ISSUES

Certain unusual religious practices affect public health, safety, and welfare, leading to additional wrinkles in the definition and allowable limits of free exercise. In 1976 a Tennessee minister from the Holiness Church of God in Jesus appealed to the State Supreme Court to let him use poisonous snakes during religious services. He told the court that he needed to handle and exhibit the snakes, as he believed that these practices confirmed God's word. The court did not challenge the minister's beliefs but upheld a local law against snake handling. The court said that "in a crowded church, with many children present, poisonous snakes posed 'a clear and present danger.' "[36]

In the 1982 case *United States v. Lee*, the U.S. Supreme Court cited public policy as its reason for not granting an exemption to an Amish man who refused to pay Social Security taxes. The Amish do not buy or file claims for any kind of health or life insurance, believing that doing so shows a lack of faith in God's providence. Community members help those in need. The Court said that too many problems would arise in trying to grant special exemptions from the tax. Society's interest in a sound tax system did not permit this type of free exercise.[37]

SABBATH OBSERVANCES

Congress also deals with free-exercise issues. A year after the *Sherbert* case was decided, the Civil Rights Act of 1964 went into effect. It protects a worker's observance of his or her Sabbath as a day of rest and bans employers from discriminating against workers in terms of "all aspects of religious observance and practice, as well as belief." The idea of "accommodation" to people's religious needs underlies this provision, which also helps members of minority religious groups gain equal opportunity in the workplace. An employer must show that he or she cannot adjust to an employee's religious practices without "a serious inconvenience to the conduct of the business."[38] The Supreme Court has defined serious inconvenience as including substantial economic loss. The Court has said that when examining such cases, it will ask whether employers have made a good-faith effort to accommodate an individual's practices.

The Court further clarified the duties and rights of an employer in 1985 when it struck down a Connecticut law that said a worker could *never* be forced to work on his or her Sabbath. The Court said that avoiding work on the Sabbath is not an "absolute and unqualified right," because such rigid laws can place undue burdens on employers and fellow employees.[39]

Through the years, as the courts have considered different church-state cases, they have interpreted the words "free exercise of religion" in a fairly broad way. Although what citizens may do in the name of religion is sometimes limited, the state does not dictate what people may or may not believe. In general, courts have heeded Thomas Jefferson's 1802 comment that government power should "reach actions only, and not opinions."

SUNDAY CLOSING LAWS

Many church-state issues touch upon both religion clauses: free exercise and establishment of religion. One such issue involves Sunday closing laws.

Some states enforce laws that require certain businesses to close on Sunday. In 1961, the Supreme Court said that Sunday closing laws are constitutional, meaning that states can legally set aside a day for rest and leisure. The Court agreed that Sunday closing laws were originally enacted to promote church attendance but said that today these laws have sound nonreligious goals: "People of all religions and people of no religion regard Sunday as a time for family activity, for visiting friends and relatives, for late sleeping, for passive and active entertainment, for dining out and the like."[40]

In another 1961 case, *Braunfeld v. Brown*, the Court examined a Pennsylvania Sunday closing law. Orthodox Jews had brought the case because they suffered economic losses by observing their own Sabbath from sundown on Friday until sundown on Saturday, then having to close again on Sunday. This time the Court upheld the state law, distinguishing between laws that forbid a religious practice and laws designed for the general welfare that put certain groups at a disadvantage because of the groups' special practices.

Justice Potter Stewart dissented, saying that the plaintiffs faced a "cruel choice" between their religious beliefs and economic survival.[41]

Because most Americans observe the Sabbath on Sunday, Sunday closing laws can be viewed as establishing their beliefs as the standard and aiding their free exercise in preference to the practices of minority religions. People who favor strict church-state separation say that such laws show a government preference for certain religions over others. Other people believe that Sunday laws serve nonreligious functions—since Sunday is a commonly recognized day of rest and recreation—and that the religious features are incidental.

9

CURRENT TRENDS AND CONTROVERSIES

Americans have lived with the Bill of Rights, including the First Amendment religion clauses, for more than two centuries. Citizens and judges have debated difficult, often emotional, questions involving the separation of church and state. Some of today's most controversial issues involve religion and politics, religion and public schools, and the role of the Supreme Court in interpreting the Constitution. Because the United States is the most religiously diverse country in the world, people are also looking for ways to find common ground.

A MOMENT OF SILENCE IN PUBLIC SCHOOLS?

In the 1985 case *Wallace v. Jaffree* (see Chapter 5), the Supreme Court said that a state law permitting a moment of silence in public schools may be constitutional, depending upon the wording of the statute and the intent of the law. The Alabama statute at issue in *Jaffree* included the phrase "for meditation or voluntary prayer." When the Court looked at this wording and studied the history of the Alabama law, it concluded that the main purpose of the statute was to promote and endorse prayer.[1]

Other states have passed moment-of-silence statutes. Should they be upheld? In 1987, *Christianity Today* published a debate in which two people gave opposing views. At issue was a New Jersey moment-of-silence law enacted in 1982. Speaking for the Christian Legal Society, attorney Heidi Hagerman supported the law as a reasonable accommodation to the religious practices of students. She pointed out that such moments can help to quiet students at the start of the school day. Hagerman acknowledged that students may already pray silently in school whenever they wish, but called scheduled moments a "forum that enables certain students to choose to meet their own religious needs." The state would overstep its role only if it were to become "a proponent of prayer and begin to promote religious activity," claimed Hagerman.[2]

Representing Americans United for Separation of Church and State, the Reverend Dr. Robert L. Maddox said, "A moment of silence designed strictly for students to get ready to begin the school day does not pose a problem."[3] But Dr. Maddox voiced concern that a state agency might design such statutes in order to establish religious activities in schools. Maddox had studied the New Jersey law and concluded that its goal was to insert prayer into public schools.

Asked whether banning a moment of silence would lead people to think that government is hostile toward religion, Maddox said that schools can avoid this problem by teaching more about religion: "Teachers and textbooks need to pay more attention to the sweep of religion and religious freedom in the United States. During the religious seasons of the year, we don't object to teachers saying, 'Here is a season that Jews, Catholics, Protestants, or Hindus regard as important and here is the meaning of it.'"[4]

SCHOOL BIBLE CLUBS

When the Supreme Court ruled, in 1990, that Bible clubs could meet in high schools after classes, their decision was based on the Equal Access Law of 1984. The law includes three provisions: first, that schools must treat student groups equally, not discriminating on the basis of religion, politics, philosophy, or the content of their speech; second, that the meetings should be initiated and led by students rather than by school officials; third, that the school has a right to maintain order and to protect the safety of students and faculty.

In the wake of the 1990 case *Westside Community Schools v. Mergens* (see Chapter 1), people are asking how schools will implement the decision, what kinds of clubs will be allowed to meet, and who can attend the meetings.

When the Equal Access Act was first proposed, some people thought it was an attempt to place religious activities in schools. The act and the *Mergens* decision are controversial. The American Civil Liberties Union said in 1990 that religious clubs in schools are an establishment of religion. School officials have expressed concern about the kinds of clubs that might demand equal access—for example, white-supremacy groups and unpopular cults.

Other people approve the *Mergens* decision. "The big difference is who is doing the praying," said Dean Kelley, a spokesman for the National Council of Churches. "When a school sponsors the prayer, it is an establishment of religion. But when students want to organize a religion club in extracurricular time, the school should get out of the way."[5]

In the months following the Bible club decision, groups such as the Campus Crusade for Christ and the Fellowship of Christian Athletes were discussing plans to develop more chapters in schools around the country. What other groups will demand equal access? How will schools, parents, and students handle the problems that result?

RELIGION AND POLITICS

It has been said that politics and religion don't mix. Yet politicians and voters are people whose religious beliefs and values may influence their decisions. How does separation of church and state work in this area of people's lives? In theory, a person cannot be kept from holding public office based on his or her religious affiliation. In 1961, the Supreme Court ruled that states cannot require oaths declaring a belief in God.[6] But religion has been an important issue in many local and national elections.

In 1960, John F. Kennedy became the first non-Protestant U.S. president. Kennedy, a Catholic, confronted the church-state issue during his campaign, saying that he would resign from office if his religion and the presidential oath ever came into conflict.[7] This direct approach is thought to have reassured voters who feared that Catholic clergy would influence government policies. During Kennedy's term, his religion was not a major concern.

Previous presidents had tended to keep their religious views private. Many attended church regularly but without fanfare. Former president Gerald Ford, a lifelong active Episcopalian, has said, "I feel very strongly that one's religious convictions are personal.... I never tried to mix religion with politics."[8]

However, in recent elections, politics and religion have been combined. During the 1980s, campaigns were organized against politicians who held views different from those of the religious groups that opposed them. Some candidates, endorsed by religious groups, called their opponents "ungodly"; others claimed that God endorsed their campaigns.[9] In 1984, groups from the so-called religious right issued report cards for various candidates, and one magazine published a Presidential Biblical Scoreboard.[10]

The rise in religious influences in politics coincided with a rise in membership in conservative churches and strong interest in television ministries. Richard G. Hutcheson, Jr., author of *God in the White House*, says that after the moral turmoil of the 1960s, these events may signify a belief that "public morality is rooted in religion."[11] However, groups like People for the American Way, a nonprofit civil liberties organization, express concern about slogans that ask voters to "send another Christian to Congress" and "take territory for our Lord Jesus Christ."[12]

Because values and beliefs do affect political choices, James Castelli, who has written numerous books and articles on religious issues, says the question "is not whether to mix religion and politics but how."[13] For example, it has been suggested that religious groups should speak only about issues and should not endorse particular candidates. But what issues are fair game? Observers note that many people do not mind if clergymen address problems like violence or racism, yet criticize these same religious leaders for publicly expressing their views on birth control or abortion.

A. James Reichley, a writer associated with the Brookings Institution, a nonpartisan think tank in Washington, D.C., is among those who say that democracy permits—and indeed should welcome—the moral insights of religious groups on ethical matters. He says, "The larger society must hope that the churches will express their positions on issues of this kind with due regard for the rights of citizens who do not share their convictions and for the continued viability of the democratic process."[14]

People for the American Way suggests these campaign guidelines: "Don't ask people to vote for you just because of your religion—or to vote against your opponent just because of his or hers. Don't claim that God endorses your candidacy or the Bible supports your platform. And don't question the personal morality of your opponents on the basis of their political views."[15] The Reverend Dr. Robert L. Maddox says, "My commitment to separation of church and state in no way precludes my active involvement in political life. Indeed, my religious commitments push me to look carefully at government and to question political leaders.... The manner in which the clergy speak and act requires skill and sensitivity, especially in these present days. By taking thought, we can maintain church-state separation and responsible citizenship."[16]

SEPARATION: A MATTER OF DEGREE

Church and state have never been totally separated in America. There have been exceptions and accommodations, including government funding of military and prison chaplains, tax exemptions for religious property, aid for parochial school students in the form of transportation and supplies, and tax deductions for those who give money to religious organizations. Practically speaking, church and state cannot be totally separate. Houses of worship and religious schools depend on local police and fire departments and other community services. Religious bodies must file deeds and other legal papers.

Certain ceremonies and symbols in American

life reflect the nation's religious heritage. The phrase "under God" is part of the flag salute; "in God we trust" appears on coins. The courts have not banned such historically rooted symbols and observances, judging them to be no major threat to civil liberties. In many church-state decisions, Supreme Court justices have taken care to express the respect that they as individuals hold toward religion. The U.S. Supreme Court is the highest legal arena for settling church-state questions, so the viewpoints of those who serve on the Court and their approaches to interpreting the Constitution determine how conflicts are resolved.

INTERPRETING THE FIRST AMENDMENT

When interpreting the First Amendment in light of today's issues, some people say that it is vital to determine "original intent"—in other words, what did the framers of the Constitution mean when they wrote the amendment? Supreme Court opinions through the years show that the justices have often considered the intent of the framers. They have used their understanding of American history and of the framers' intentions to back up their decisions.

Many historians say that the people who wrote the First Amendment did not agree among themselves. The framers who wrote the Bill of Rights and the citizens who ratified it may have had different views about what the First Amendment meant. An attorney and expert on the First Amendment, Leo Pfeffer, is among those who say that "the discovery of any universal intent...is close to impossible."[17] The actions of the nation's first presidents show differences of opinion: Washington and Adams declared national days of prayer, while Jefferson and Madison did not. Washington believed it was legal to fund military chaplains, but Madison and Jefferson did not, nor would they support laws exempting religious property from taxation.

Members of the Supreme Court also hold different views on interpreting the First Amendment. Justice Wiley Rutledge, who served on the Court during the 1940s, said, "We have staked the very existence of our country on the faith that the complete separation between the state and religion is best for the state and best for religion."[18] In 1947, Justice Hugo Black said, "The First Amendment has erected a wall between church and state. That wall must be kept high and impregnable. We would not approve the slightest breach."[19] Five years later his colleague Justice Felix Frankfurter said, "Government should not be allowed, under cover of the soft euphemism of 'cooperation,' to steal into the sacred area of religious choice."[20]

On the other hand, William O. Douglas, a justice from 1939 to 1975, said, "We are a religious people whose institutions presuppose a Supreme Being.... When the state encourages religious instruction or cooperates with religious authorities...it follows the best of our traditions."[21] Such a view might have come from one of the Court's more conservative members today. Oddly, Douglas later became known as one of the most liberal Court members.

Supporters of "original intent"—usually political conservatives—often argue for judicial restraint, believing that the Court should play a more limited role in interpreting laws. They think that in recent decades the Court has been too active and should leave states and communities more power to determine local practices. Chief Justice William Rehnquist has expressed this view, saying in 1985 that strict separation between church and states goes against the First Amendment. Rehnquist called Thomas Jefferson's "wall of separation" phrase "a metaphor based on bad history...which has proved worthless as a guide to judging" and should be "abandoned."[22] Another member of the Court, Justice Anthony Kennedy, said in 1989 that when the courts try to maintain absolute separation between church and state, they appear to show hostility and disapproval toward religion.[23] Justice Antonin Scalia agrees with Rehnquist and Kennedy that the Court should take a less active role in making law, permitting more cooperation between government and religion. These justices have said that government can give nonpreferential aid to religion—that is, aid that is given impartially to all groups, without favoritism.[24]

In spite of differences of opinion on what the First Amendment says and what the role of the Supreme Court should be and how it should interpret the First Amendment, cases must be resolved, whether or not those who wrote the amendment had a clear intent. Even if such an intent could be found, should it bind those who must resolve today's church-state conflicts? Justice Byron White, appointed in 1962, explained, "In the end, the courts have fashioned answers to these questions as best they can, the language and its history having left them a wide range of choice...and in choosing, the courts necessarily have carved out what they deemed to be the most desirable national policy governing various aspects of church-state relationships."[25] According to constitutional expert Leonard Levy, "we are bound to consider only whether the purposes they [the framers] had in mind still merit political respect and constitutional obedience. History can only be a guide, not a controlling factor."[26] Levy offers a strict interpretation of the First Amendment when he writes, "At bottom the amendment was an expression of the fact that the framers of the Constitution had not intended to empower Congress to act in the field of religion. To Madison and others it was one of the 'forbidden fields of government.'"[27]

In 1985, Justice John Paul Stevens summarized how ways of looking at liberty of conscience have evolved through the years:

> *At one time, it was thought that this right merely proscribed the preference of one Christian sect over another, but would not require equal respect for the conscience of the infidel, the atheist, or the adherent of a non-Christian faith such as Mohammedism or Judaism. But when the underlying principle has been examined...the Court has unambiguously concluded that the individual freedom of conscience protected by the First Amendment embraces the right to select any religious faith or none at all. This conclusion derives support not only from the interest in respecting the individual's freedom of conscience but also from the conviction that religious beliefs worthy of respect are the product of free and voluntary choice.*[28]

LIVING WITH RELIGIOUS DIFFERENCES

Today's United States is quite different from that of 1791, when the Bill of Rights was written. Then the U.S. population consisted of not quite 3 million, mostly Protestant, citizens. Today the nation spreads from coast to coast and has a diverse population of nearly 270 million people. Government is involved in many activities, such as public education, that did not exist in 1791. There may be as many as three thousand different religious groups in the United States.[29] Many citizens voice no religious affiliation. The American system permits all to hold their own beliefs.

More than a million people have sought religious freedom in America during the past two centuries. Although most of today's immigrants do not come for religious reasons, some do. This desire for freedom—for those fundamental rights set forth in the Bill of Rights—connects Americans of diverse backgrounds.

In 1988, more than two hundred prominent Americans from many areas of public life approved the Williamsburg Charter, which commemorates the religious liberty clauses of the Bill of Rights. The charter, signed by people with diverse religious and political views, admits that Americans have ongoing differences and that "differences over belief are the deepest and least easily negotiated of all."[30] Nonetheless, the people who signed the charter agreed upon these principles: "Religious liberty in a democracy is a right that may not be submitted to vote.... A society is only as just and free as it is respectful of this right, especially toward the beliefs of its smallest minorities and least popular communities.... We affirm that a right for one is a right for another and a responsibility for all."[31] A summary of the charter's principles can be found in the Appendix.

Former Supreme Court Justice Robert H. Jackson once said, "The very purpose of a Bill of Rights was to withdraw certain subjects from the vicissitudes of political controversy, to place them beyond the reach of majorities and officials.... One's right to life, liberty, and property, to free speech, a free press, freedom to worship and assemble, and other fundamental rights may not be submitted to a vote; they depend on the outcome of no elections."[32]

Religious liberty, based upon the concept of the separation of church and state, depends on the outcome of no election. It offers America, the most pluralistic—that is, diverse—society in history an important tool for maintaining mutual respect.

How has it fared, this American experiment with religious liberty? America has not suffered from the widespread religious wars or the official persecutions that have troubled some countries. For example, Catholics and Protestants have been warring in Northern Ireland for years, and old religious conflicts long suppressed by communist governments in Eastern Europe are surfacing in ugly new ways. In some countries, majority religions either have established themselves or are attempting to establish themselves as the state religion. In other countries, religious groups and factions, which also are usually ethnic groups, are vying for political and economic power—in India, Iraq, Israel, and Armenia, to name just four places.

Church membership and attendance at worship services in the United States are among the highest in the world. Other countries have observed and sometimes have imitated the American effort to provide freedom of conscience through separation of church and state. They have watched Americans work to apply the principles in the Constitution to everyday situations. Alvin W. Johnson and Frank H. Yost, authors of *Separation of Church and State in the United States*, conclude that the First Amendment religion clauses have made an important contribution both in the United States and abroad: "A new nation with the old religious despotism still clinging to it would have been no great addition to the world's assets, but a nation founded upon the true principles of both civil and religious liberty was indeed a noteworthy achievement."[33]

Although liberty cannot be taken for granted because of a document written two hundred years ago, the idea of separation of church and state, outlined in the Constitution and adapted to a changing society, represents a gallant attempt to resolve in day-to-day life those deep religious differences that are part of what we are as a nation.

APPENDIX:
THE WILLIAMSBURG CHARTER

SUMMARY OF PRINCIPLES

"Congress shall make no law respecting an establishment of religion, or prohibiting the free exercise thereof..."

The Religious Liberty clauses of the First Amendment to the Constitution are a momentous decision, the most important political decision for religious liberty and public justice in history. Two hundred years after their enactment they stand out boldly in a century made dark by state repression and sectarian conflict. Yet the ignorance and contention now surrounding the clauses are a reminder that their advocacy and defense is a task for each succeeding generation.

We acknowledge our deep and continuing differences over religious beliefs, political policies and constitutional interpretations. But together we celebrate the genius of the Religious Liberty clauses, and affirm the following truths to be among the first principles that are in the shared interest of all Americans:

1. Religious liberty, or freedom of conscience, is a precious, fundamental and inalienable right. A society is only as just and free as it is respectful of this right for its smallest minorities and least popular communities.

2. Religious liberty is founded on the inviolable dignity of the person. It is not based on science or social usefulness and is not dependent on the shifting moods of majorities and governments.

3. Religious liberty is our nation's "first liberty," which undergirds all other rights and freedoms secured by the Bill of Rights.

4. The two Religious Liberty clauses address distinct concerns, but together they serve the same end—religious liberty, or freedom of conscience, for citizens of all faiths or none.

5. The No Establishment clause separates Church from State but not religion from politics or public life. It prevents the confusion of religion and government which has been a leading source of repression and coercion throughout history.

6. The Free Exercise clause guarantees the right to reach, hold, exercise or change beliefs freely. It allows all citizens who so desire to shape their lives, whether private or public, on the basis of personal and communal beliefs.

7. The Religious Liberty clauses are both a protection of individual liberty and a provision for ordering the relationship of religion and public life. They allow us to live with our deepest differences and enable diversity to be a source of national strength.

8. Conflict and debate are vital to democracy. Yet if controversies about religion and politics are to reflect the highest wisdom of the First Amendment and advance the best interests of the disputants and the nation, then *how* we debate, and not only *what* we debate, is critical.

9. One of America's continuing needs is to develop, out of our differences, a common vision for the common good. Today that common vision must embrace a shared understanding of the place of religion in public life and of the guiding principles by which people with deep religious differences can contend robustly but civilly with each other.

10. Central to the notion of the common good, and of greater importance each day because of the increase of pluralism, is the recognition that religious liberty is a

universal right joined to a universal duty to respect the right. Rights are best guarded and responsibilities best exercised when each person and group guards for all others those rights they wish guarded for themselves.

We are firmly persuaded that these principles require a fresh consideration, and that the reaffirmation of religious liberty is crucial to sustain a free people that would remain free. We therefore commit ourselves to speak, write and act according to this vision and these principles. We urge our fellow citizens to do the same, now and in generations to come.

SOURCE NOTES

CHAPTER 1
1. Kevin Sack, "School Mural: Sociology or Religion?" *New York Times*, 1 May 1990, B-1.
2. Ibid., B-4.
3. Westside Board of Education v. Mergens, No. 88-1597.
4. Leo Pfeffer, *The Liberties of an American* (Boston: The Beacon Press, 1956), p. 31.
5. Davis v. Beason 133 U.S. 333 (1890) in Anson Phelps Stokes and Leo Pfeffer, *Church and State in the United States* (New York: Harper and Row, 1964), p. 110.
6. Everson v. Board of Education, 330 U.S. 1 (1947) 67 S. Ct. 504 in Frank J. Sorauf, *The Wall of Separation* (Princeton, N.J.: Princeton University Press, 1976), pp. 19–20.
7. Robert Maddox, "The Ramparts Besieged," *The Christian Century*, 25 February 1987, p. 191.
8. Wallace v. Jaffree, 105 S. Ct. 2520.
9. Quoted in Vashti McCollum, *One Woman's Fight* (Boston: Beacon Press, 1953) p. 174.

CHAPTER 2
1. Jerome G. Kerwin, *Catholic Viewpoint on Church and State* (Garden City, N.Y.: Hanover House, 1960), p. 40.
2. Leo Pfeffer, *Church, State, and Freedom* (Boston: Beacon Press, 1953), pp.15–16.

3. Everson v. Board of Education, in Robert S. Alley, *The Supreme Court on Church and State* (New York: Oxford University Press, 1988), pp. 41–42.

4. William Warren Sweet, *Religion in Colonial America* (New York: Cooper Square, 1965), p. 322.

5. Charles M. Andrews, *The Colonial Period in American History: The Settlements* (New Haven: Yale University Press, 1936), p. 318.

6. Margaret Hope Bacon, *The Quiet Rebels: The Story of the Quakers in America* (Philadelphia: New Society, 1985) p. 37.

7. Leonard W. Levy, *The Establishment Clause: Religion and the First Amendment* (New York: Macmillan, 1986), p. 10.

8. Pfeffer, *Church, State, and Freedom*, pp. 17–18.

9. Jerry H. Combee, "Evangelicals and the First Amendment," *National Review*, 24 October 1986, p. 40.

10. Albert J. Menendez, *The Origins of Religious Liberty* (Silver Spring, Md.: Americans United Research Foundation, 1976), p. 7.

11. Anson Phelps Stokes and Leo Pfeffer, *Church and State in the United States* (New York: Harper and Row, 1964), p. 13.

12. Sydney E. Ahlstrom, *A Religious History of the American People* (New Haven, Conn.: Yale University Press, 1972), p. 168.

13. "Roger Williams, Prophet of Freedom," *Church & State*, June 1975, pp. 4–5

14. Stokes and Pfeffer, pp. 7–8.

15. Pfeffer, *Church, State, and Freedom*, p. 74.

16. Milton Meltzer, *Ain't Gonna Study War No More* (New York: Harper and Row, 1985), p. 35.

17. Lillian Barr, Unpublished Master's Thesis, University of Chicago, 1920, in Sweet, p. 163.

18. Pfeffer, *Church, State, and Freedom*, pp. 90–91.

19. Glenn T. Miller, *Religious Liberty in America* (Philadelphia: Westminster Press, 1976), p. 57.

20. Albert Q. Maisel, *They All Chose America* (New York: Thomas Nelson and Sons, 1957), p. 154.

21. Ibid.
22. Pfeffer, *Church, State, and Freedom*, p. 85, and Sweet, pp. 146–147.
23. Richard N. Current et al., *Words That Made American History* (Boston: Little, Brown, 1972), p. 86.
24. Pfeffer, *Liberties of an American*, p. 35.

CHAPTER 3
1. Robert S. Alley, ed., *James Madison on Religious Liberty* (Buffalo, N.Y.: Prometheus Books, 1985), p. 24.
2. Ibid.
3. Thomas Jefferson, *Notes on Virginia*, in Stokes and Pfeffer, p. 53.
4. Ibid.
5. James Madison, "Memorial and Remonstrance Against Religious Assessments," June 20, 1785, in Robert S. Alley, *The Supreme Court on Church and State* (New York: Oxford University Press, 1988), p. 19.
6. Ibid., p. 18.
7. Stokes and Pfeffer, p. 52.
8. Ibid., p. 62.
9. Leonard W. Levy, *Original Intent and the Framers' Constitution* (New York: Macmillan, 1988), p. 176.
10. Leonard Levy, *Judgments: Essays on American Constitutional History* (Chicago: Quadrangle Books, 1972), p. 184.
11. Ibid., p. 231.
12. Saul K. Padover, *The Complete Jefferson* (New York: Duell, Sloan, & Pearce, 1943), pp. 518–519.
13. Richard E. Morgan, *The Supreme Court and Religion* (New York: The Free Press, 1972), pp. 30–31, and Stokes and Pfeffer, pp. 78–82.
14. Pfeffer, *Church, State, and Freedom*, p. 543.
15. Alexis de Tocqueville, *Democracy in America*, ed. J. P. Mayer, trans. George Lawrence (Garden City, N.Y.: Doubleday, 1969), p. 295.

CHAPTER 4

1. Menendez, p. 29.
2. Rabbi Arthur Gilbert, *A Jew in Christian America* (New York: Sheed and Ward, 1966), p. 130, and Boardman W. Kathan, "Prayer and the Public Schools: The Issue in Historical Perspective and Implications for Religious Education Today," *Religious Education*, Spring 1989 (Vol. 84, No. 2), p. 243.
3. Samuel Rabinove, "Religious Liberty and Church-State Separation," *Vital Speeches of the Day*, 15 June 1986, p. 527.
4. Charles C. Haynes, *Religion in American History* (Alexandria, Va: Association for Supervision and Curriculum Development, 1990), p. 99.
5. Gilbert, pp. 136–37.
6. Stokes and Pfeffer, pp. 106–107.

CHAPTER 5

1. Board of Education of Cincinnati v. Minor, 23 Ohio St. 211 (1872) in Alvin W. Johnson and Frank H. Yost, *Separation of Church and State in the United States* (New York: Greenwood Press, 1948). p. 30.
2. People ex. rel. Ring v. Board of Education of District 24, 245 Ill. 334 (1910).
3. "School Bible Reading Survey," *Church & State*, January 1960, p. 5.
4. School District of Abington Township v. Schempp, 374 U.S. 203 (1963), in Alley, *The Supreme Court of Church and State*, pp. 214–216, and Murray v. Curlett 374 U.S. 203 (1963), in Milton R. Konvitz, *Expanding Liberties: Freedom's Gains in Postwar America* (New York: Viking Press, 1966), p. 31.
5. School District of Abington Township v. Schempp, 374 U.S. 203, (1963) Footnote 60.
6. Illinois ex. rel. McCollum v. Board of Education, 333 U.S. 203 (1948) in Alley, p. 177.
7. Concurring opinion in Illinois ex. rel. McCollum v. Board of Education, in McCollum, p. 81.
8. McCollum, p. 98.

9. Ibid., p. 10.
10. Ibid., p. 14.
11. Ibid., p. 19.
12. Zorach v. Clausen 343 U.S. 306 (1952) in Alley, p. 193.
13. Fred W. Friendly and Martha J. H. Elliot, *The Constitution: That Delicate Balance* (New York: Random House, 1984), p. 121.
14. Engel v. Vitale 370 U.S. 421 (1962) in Alley, *The Supreme Court on Church and State*, pp. 200–201.
15. Ibid.
16. Friendly, p. 125.
17. *Public Papers of the Presidents of the United States: John F. Kennedy, 1962* (Washington, D.C.: U.S. Government Printing Office), pp. 510–511.
18. Peter Irons, T*he Courage of Their Convictions* (New York: The Free Press, 1988), p. 362.
19. Ibid., p. 365.
20. Wallace v. Jaffree 105 S. Ct. 2479 (1985) quoted in Levy, *The Establishment Clause, op. cit.,* pp. 150–151.
21. Irons, p. 375.
22. "Silent Prayer: The Press Speaks Out," *Church and State*, July–August 1985, p. 13.
23. Ibid.
24. Jim Buie, "The Supreme Court Verdict on School Prayer," *Church and State*, July–August 1985, p.12.
25. Ibid., p. 14.
26. Ibid.
27. Hayne, p. 143.
28. Rabinove, p. 528.
29. Bill Wilburn, "Prayers Ignore Court Ban," *Christianity Today*, 3 November 1989, p. 38.
30. United Presbyterians, "Relations Between Church and State," 175th General Assembly, May 1963, in Konvitz, p. 38.
31. Rob Boston, "Christmas Carols Get a Frosty Reception in Florida Public Schools," *Church & State*, December 1988, p. 11.
32. "Religious Holidays in the Public Schools," Pamphlet:

Americans United for the Separation of Church and State (Silver Spring, Md.: n.d.).

CHAPTER 6

1. Irons, p. 210.
2. Epperson v. Arkansas, 393 U.S. 97 (1968), quoted in Isidore Starr, "Teetering on the Wall of Separation," in Charles Haynes, *Religious Freedom in America* (Silver Spring, Md.: Americans United Research Foundation, 1986), p. 46.
3. Irons, pp. 216–223.
4. Paul Weingarten, "Texas Takes on the E-Word in Seeking Textbook Change," *Chicago Tribune*, 13 February 1989.
5. McClain v. Arkansas Board of Education quoted in Maddox, *Separation of Church and State*, p. 169; and Irons, p. 216.
6. Edwards v. Aguillard, 107 S. Ct. 2573 (1987) in Alley, *The Supreme Court on Church and State*, pp. 258–261.
7. Ibid.
8. Seth Mydans, "In a Small Town a Battle Over a Book," *New York Times*, 3 September 1989, in *People for the American Way: Press Clips*, July–August–September, 1989, p. 8.
9. Ibid.
10. Marilyn Elias, "Censorship Is Gaining in Schools," *USA Today,* 31 August 1989, in *People for the American Way: Press Clips*. July–August–September, 1989, p. 10.
11. "Fundamentalists Abandon Secular Humanism Crusade in Court," *Church & State*, January, 1988, p. 13.
12. Robert Engleman, "Religion Not Going Down in History," *San Jose Mercury-News*, 31 May 1986, in *People for the American Way: Press Clips*, April–May–June 1986, p. 25.
13. Ibid.
14. Abington v. Schempp, in Alley, *The Supreme Court on Church and State*, p. 215.

15. "Holiday Guidelines," *Christianity Today*, 17 November 1987, p. 70.

Chapter 7

1. Walz v. Tax Commission, 397 U.S. 664 (1970) in Alley, *The Supreme Court on Church and State*, p. 83.
2. "States May Tax Bible Sales (Supreme Court Ruling)," *Christianity Today*, 19 February 1990, p. 37.
3. "Should Tax Dollars Finance Parochial Schools?" Pamphlet, Americans United for the Separation of Church and State (Silver Spring, Md.: n.d.).
4. Lemon v. Kurtzman, 91 S. Ct. 2105 (1971) in Haynes, *Religious Freedom in America*, p. 49.
5. Dee Maggiori, "State's Catholic School Parents Form Federation," *Fairfield County Catholic*, August 1990, p. 1.
6. Levy, *The Establishment Clause*, p. 134.
7. Shane P. Martin, "Is Catholic Education Providing Something Public Schools Cannot?" *America*, 26 May 1990, pp. 520–522.
8. Joseph L. Conn, "The Supreme Court Verdict on Parochaid," *Church & State*, July–August 1985, pp. 4–7.
9. J. M. Dawson, *America's Way in Church, State, and Society* (New York: Macmillan, 1953), p. 69.
10. Thomas Jefferson, *Bill For Establishing Religious Freedom*, in Pfeffer, *Church, State, and Freedom*, p. 101.
11. Lynch v. Donnelly 465 U.S. 668 (1984), in Alley, *The Supreme Court on Church and State*, p. 320.
12. Ibid., pp. 321–322.
13. Ibid., pp. 323–324.
14. Rob Boston, "Away With the Manger?" *Church & State*, December 1988, p. 9.
15. Rob Boston, "When Symbols Clash," *Church & State*, September 1989, p. 9.
16. Ibid., p. 9.
17. Ibid., p. 9.
18. Ibid., p. 11.

19. "Sectarian Symbols at City Hall: What the Press said," *Church & State*, September 1989), p. 11.
20. Ibid., p. 11.
21. Maddox, *Separation of Church and State*, p. 175.

CHAPTER 8
1. Reynolds v. United States, 98 U.S. 145 (1878), in Stokes and Pfeffer, pp. 108–109.
2. Davis v. Beason, 133 U.S. 333 (1890), in Stokes and Pfeffer, *Church and State in the United States*, p. 110.
3. In re: Church of Jesus Christ of Latter-Day Saints, in Stokes and Pfeffer, p. 111.
4. Sherbert v. Verner, 374 U.S. 398 (1963), in Leonard F. Manning, *The Law of Church-State Relations* (St. Paul, Minn.: West Publishing, 1981), pp. 274–275.
5. *Minutes Magazine* (Nationwide Insurance Co., Columbus, Ohio, n.d.), unpaged.
6. Milton Meltzer, *Ain't Gonna Study War No More*, p. 26.
7. Ibid., pp. 46–47.
8. Ibid., p. 47.
9. Ibid., p. 50.
10. William O. Douglas, *The Right of the People* (Garden City, New York: Doubleday, 1958), pp. 142–143.
11. Ibid., p. 143.
12. United States v. Seeger, 380 U.S. 163 (1965), in William Lee Miller, *The First Liberty* (New York: Knopf, 1985), pp. 336–338.
13. Douglas, p. 143.
14. In Michael P. Showalter, "The Flag Salute Cases," *Cobblestone*, March 1989, p. 23.
15. Gilbert, p. 133.
16. Leonard A. Stevens, *Salute! The Case of the Bible vs. the Flag* (New York: Coward, McCann, and Geoghan, 1973), p. 25.
17. Minersville School District v. Gobitis, 310 U.S. 586 (1940), in Alley, *The Supreme Court on Church and State*, pp. 365–371. Note: The name "Gobitas" was misspelled as "Gobitis" in court records.
18. Ibid., p. 374.

19. Stevens, p. 17.
20. West Virginia State Board of Education v. Barnette, 319 U.S. 624 (1943) in Stokes and Pfeffer, pp. 124–125.
21. Irons, p. 25.
22. Ibid., p. 35.
23. Wisconsin v. Yoder, 406 U.S. 205 (1972), in Manning, pp. 278–279.
24. "Only Adults Can Refuse Medical Care, says Mass. High Court in Jehovah's Witness Blood Transfusion Case," *Church & State*, March 1991, p. 22.
25. John Sexton and Nat Brandt, *How Free Are We?* (New York: M. Evans, 1986), pp. 172–73.
26. "Trial of Christian Scientists in Son's Death Goes to Jury," *New York Times,* 3 July 1990, A-15.
27. Ibid.
28. American Indian Religious Freedom Act of 1978 (AIRFA), in "A History of the American Indian Religious Freedom Act and Its Implementation," *Indian Affairs* (Special Supplement), Summer 1988.
29. Reginald Johnson, "Ancient Rights: State's Indians Fight for Respect and Recogntion," *Fairpress* (Fairfield, Conn.), 26 April 1990, A-1.
30. Rob Boston, "The Day Sherbert Melted," *Church & State*, June 1990, p. 4.
31. Rob Boston, "Peyote Impasse," *Church & State,* February 1990, p. 11.
32. Ibid., p. 10.
33. Ibid., p. 11.
34. Joan Johnson, *The Cult Movement* (New York: Franklin Watts, 1984), p. 2.
35. "'Cult Influence Is Greatly Exaggerated,' says Sociologist," *Church & State*, January 1988, pp. 13–14.
36. Sexton and Brandt, pp. 171–2.
37. Ibid.
38. Isidore Starr, p. 45.
39. Jim Buie, "Connecticut Sabbath Law Remembered the Sabbath but not the Constitution," *Church & State*, July–August 1985, p. 10.

40. McGowan v. Maryland, 366 U.S. 420 (1961), in
Alley, *The Supreme Court on Church and State*,
pp. 280–289.
41. Braunfeld v. Brown, 366 U.S. 599 (1961) in Alley, *The
Supreme Court on Church and State*, pp. 402–405.

CHAPTER 9
1. Wallace v. Jaffree, *op. cit.*
2. "Can a State Require Public Schools to Allow
a Moment of Silence?" *Christianity Today*,
20 November 1987, p. 52.
3. Ibid.
4. Ibid.
5. Alain L. Sanders, "Prayers in the Schoolhouse,"
Time, 15 January 1990, p. 51.
6. Torcaso v. Watkins, 367 U.S. 488 (1961) in Manning,
pp. 280–281.
7. Richard G. Hutcheson, Jr., *God in the White House*
(New York: Macmillan, 1988), p. 53.
8. Ibid. p. 52.
9. Kate DeSmet, "Pat Robertson Isn't God's Candidate,
Minister Says," *Detroit News*, 27 September 1986, in
People for the American Way: Press Clips,
October–November–December 1986, p. 19.
10. John Buchanan and Barbara Jordan, "Connecting
People's Politics and God Is Wrong," *Houston Post*,
15 May 1986, in *People for the American Way: Press
Clips*, April–May–June, 1986, p. 1.
11. Hutcheson, p. x.
12. Buchanan and Jordan, p. 1.
13. Quoted in George Higgins, "JFK on Church and
State," *America*, 5 May 1990, p. 452.
14. Quoted in George Higgins, "JFK on Church and
State," *America*, 5 May 1990, p. 454.
15. People for the American Way, "Election Project—
Questions and Answers" (pamphlet), 1988.
16. Robert L. Maddox, *Separation of Church and State*
(New York: Crossroad, 1987), pp. 8–9.
17. Pfeffer, *Liberties of an American*, p. 26.
18. Starr, p. 33.

19. Everson v. Board of Education 333 U.S. 1 (1947), in Frank J. Sorauf, *The Wall of Separation*, pp. 19–20.
20. Dissenting opinion in Zorach v. Clausen, 343 U.S. 204 1952, cited in Alley, *The Supreme Court on Church and State*, pp. 190–92.
21. Zorach v. Clausen, 343 U.S. 204 1952, in Alley, *The Supreme Court on Church and State*, p. 186.
22. Donald L. Drakeman, "The New Court and Church-State Issues," *Christian Century*, July 2–9, 1986, p. 608 [citing dissenting opinion in Wallace v. Jaffree, 105 S. Ct. 2479 (1985)].
23. Boston, "When Symbols Clash," p. 12.
24. Ibid.
25. Dissenting opinion: Committee for Public Education v. Nyquist, 413 U.S. 820 (1973).
26. Levy, *The Establishment Clause*, p. 175.
27. Levy, *Judgements*, pp. 186–87.
28. Wallace v. Jaffree, 105 S. Ct. 2479 (1985), in Alley, *Supreme Court on Church and State*, p. 231.
29. Maddox, *Separation of Church and State*, p. 13.
30. Samuel Rabinove, "Williamsburg Charter Fuels Debate," *The Christian Century*, 9 November 1988, p. 107.
31. Ibid.
32. West Virginia State Board of Education v. Barnette, in Alley, *The Supreme Court on Church and State*, pp. 383–384.
33. Johnson and Yost, p. 15.

FOR FURTHER READING

Alley, Robert S. *So Help Me God: Religion and the Presidency: Wilson to Nixon*. Richmond, Va.: John Knox Press, 1972.

Beggs, David W. III, and R. Bruch McQuigg. *America's Schools and Churches: Partners in Conflict*. Bloomington, Ind.: University of Indiana Press, 1965.

Berger, Raoul. *Congress v. the Supreme Court*. Boston: Harvard University Press, 1969.

Bernstein, Richard B., and Jerome Agel. *Into the Third Century: The Supreme Court*. New York: Walker, 1989.

Bowen, Catherine Drinker. *Miracle in Philadelphia: The Story of the Constitutional Convention, May to September 1787*. Boston: Atlantic Monthly Press, 1986.

Curtis, Michael Kent. *No State Shall Abridge: The Fourteenth Amendment and the Bill of Rights*. Durham, N.C.: Duke University Press, 1986.

Douglas, William O. *The Bible and the Schools*. Boston: Little, Brown, 1966.

Faber, Doris and Harold. *We The People: The Story of the Constitution Since 1787*. New York: Scribners, 1987.

Foner, Eric. *Tom Paine and Revolutionary America*. New York: Oxford University Press, 1976.

Garraty, John A., ed. *Quarrels That Have Shaped the Constitution*. New York: Harper and Row, 1975.

Gaustad, Edwin Scott. *A Religious History of America*. New York: Harper and Row, 1966.

Handlin, Oscar. *Adventure in Freedom: Three Hundred Years of Jewish Life in America*. Port Washington, N.Y.: Kennikat, 1954.

Handy, Robert T. *A Christian America: Protestant Hopes and Historical Realities*. New York: Oxford University Press, 1971.

Hill, Samuel S., and Dennis E. Owen. *The New Religious Political Right in America*. Nashville, Tenn.: Abingdon, 1982.

Holder, Angela Roddey. *The Meaning of the Constitution*. Woodbury, N.Y.: Barron's Educational Series, 1974.

Horn, Carl, ed. *Whose Values? The Battle for Morality in Pluralistic America*. Ann Arbor, Mich.: Servant Books, 1985.

Koch, Adrienne. *Jefferson and Madison: The Great Collaboration*. New York: Knopf, 1950.

Lawson, Don. *Landmark Supreme Court Cases*. Hillsdale, N.J.: Enslow, 1987.

Lieberman, Jethro K. *Milestones: 200 Years of American Law*. New York: Oxford University Press, 1976.

McCuen, Gary E. *Religion and Politics: Issues in Religious Liberty*. Hudson, Wis.: Gary E. McCuen Publications, 1989.

McConnell, Michael W. "Why 'Separation' Is Not the Key to Church-State Relations." *The Christian Century*, 18 January 1989, pp. 43–47.

Marnell, William H. *The First Amendment: The History of Religious Freedom in America*. New York: Doubleday, 1964.

Spiro, Daniel A. "Public Schools and the Road to Neutrality." *Phi Delta Kappan*, June 1989, pp. 759–63.

Tarshis, Lauren. "From High School to the High Court." *Scholastic Update*, January 26, 1990, pp. 5–7.

Tribe, Laurence H. *God Save This Honorable Court: How the Choice of Justices Can Change Our Lives*. New York: Random House, 1985.

Wiecek, William M. *Liberty Under Law: The Supreme Court in American Life*. Baltimore, Md.: Johns Hopkins University Press, 1988.

Zaretsky, Irving I., and Mark P. Leone. *Religious Movements in Contemporary America*. Princeton, N.J.: Princeton University Press, 1974.

INDEX

126